COLOR IMAGE EDITING

with

PhotoFinish

Stephen Beale

MICRO PUBLISHING PRESS
Torrance, California

Color Image Editing with PhotoFinish
Stephen Beale

Published by:
Micro Publishing Press
21150 Hawthorne Blvd., Suite 104
Torrance, CA 90503
(310) 371-5787

First Printing, September, 1993

Printed in the United States of America

ISBN 0-941845-10-9

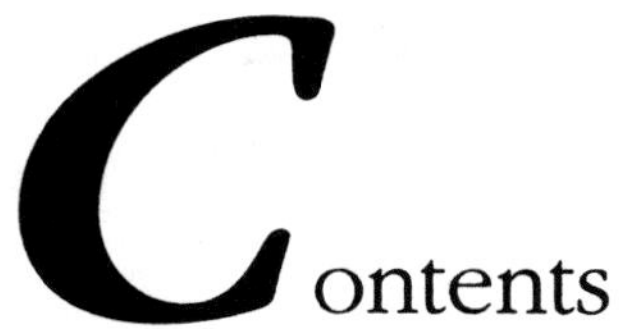ontents

Introduction

Science-fiction movies like Terminator 2 have stunned audiences worldwide with their reality-defying special effects. Taking advantage of the latest advances in computer technology, film producers can create almost any illusion that can be imagined, whether it's molten metal turned into human form or a boy on a bicycle flying through the air.

The computers used to produce these special effects are much more powerful than the PCs that sit on so many desks these days. However, for less than $200, you can now purchase a software package that lets you create a wide range of photographic effects not unlike those used by cinematic wizards.

This program is called PhotoFinish. It was developed by one of the pioneers of personal computer graphics, an Atlanta-based company called ZSoft Corp. It runs under Microsoft Windows, a "graphical operating environment" that brings to PC-compatible computers many of the user-friendly features found in Apple's Macintosh.

Programs like PhotoFinish go by many names: image-editing software, color-editing software, and so on. What they have in common is their ability to modify photographic images that have been converted into a digital format.

PhotoFinish is a productive tool for scanning, calibrating, and retouching photographs, logos, and other images that are intended for use in an electronic page layout. Though intended largely for color photos, it also works with gray-scale or line-art images. In addition to working with existing artwork, it can be used to create illustrations, logos, or other graphic elements from scratch. It is even a tool for the fine artist, who can create full-color artwork that might resemble photographic imagery—but then again might not.

Thanks to its calibration tools, PhotoFinish also provides a "glue" holding together the many components used in color publishing systems. In the days before PCs became popular as graphics tools, color publications were produced by costly proprietary prepress systems run by highly trained operators. Almost all of the components in these prepress systems were provided by a single manufacturer who made sure that they communicated with each other in a consistent and accurate manner.

With the desktop publishing revolution and the subsequent digital color publishing revolution, the production of color pages is increasingly handled by systems in which the components come from different manufacturers and software developers. A typical PC system might include a scanner, monitor, and printer from any of several dozen manufacturers. Likewise, color separations can be produced on many different imagesetters with varying reproduction characteristics.

Each of these components adds its own bias to the way color is handled. Calibration functions such as those found in PhotoFinish offer a way of modifying images to remove this bias as much as possible. Though PhotoFinish is far from being the only solution for color correction and calibration, it is certainly one of the most cost-effective.

About This Book

This is a book about PhotoFinish. Though the program is relatively easy to learn and use, color imaging is a challenging subject at best and a sorcerer's art at worst. It requires the computer user to learn a complete new set of terms and concepts. As with any new technology, it is easy for even the best and brightest to get hopelessly confused.

We hope that this book provides a way out of the confusion. More than a guide to PhotoFinish, it is intended as a general introduction to color imaging on the PC. It covers the two most recent versions of PhotoFinish, 2.0 and 3.0.

In Chapter One, "The Basics of Color Imaging," we provide a general introduction to color perception, prepress, and production. This is a complex subject deserving of an entire book in its own right. But we will try to cover the basic concepts needed to use PhotoFinish and other hardware and software components you will use in conjunction with the program.

Chapter Two, "An Introduction to PhotoFinish," is an overview of the capabilities in PhotoFinish. It describes the basic functions of the program and the file formats it supports.

Chapter Three, "PhotoFinsh Menus," is an in-depth discussion of the many menu options in PhotoFinish, with a focus on filters that can modify images in many ways.

Chapter Four, "PhotoFinish Workboxes," describes the PhotoFinish toolbox and palette, describing each of the many tools provided in the program.

Chapter Five, "Capturing Images," covers the process of bringing images into PhotoFinish. It discusses the various image-capture hardware products available to PhotoFinish users, including scanners, digitizers, and Kodak's Photo CD system. It also describes the scanner control and calibration functions in PhotoFinish and provides tips on setting your scanning parameters.

Chapter Six, "Enhancing Images," discusses color control and image correction, with a focus on the image-enhancement functions in PhotoFinish.

Chapter Seven, "Modifying Images: Step by Step," provides a detailed guide to some common image-editing functions in PhotoFinish. We will do a simple color conversion and perform some magic with a pair of unrelated photographs to create an image that defies reality—just like the movies.

Chapter Eight, "Working with Other Programs," discusses software packages that you may use in conjunction with PhotoFinish, including desktop publishing, illustration, presentation, and multimedia programs.

Finally, Chapter Nine, "Output Options," discusses the many issues involved in producing images that have been enhanced with PhotoFinish. We cover various output devices, from laser printers to PostScript imagesetters, and also provide tips on dealing with service bureaus and printers.

The Appendix provides a glossary of terms and information about products used in conjunction with PhotoFinish.

About ZSoft

When using a program, it is nice to know something about the company that created it. PhotoFinish, now officially a product of WordStar International, was originally devloped by a company called ZSoft Corp. It is descended from a proud line of graphics programs that originated in one of the first paint packages for PC-compatible computers.

ZSoft got its name from Mark Zachmann, who founded the company in what has become the "log cabin" of many software developers—his basement.

Zachmann, who had earned an M.S. degree in Operations Research from the University of Rochester, was a PhD candidate in 1981 when he began working on the IBM Personal Computer, which had just been released. Frustrated at being unable to print graphics, he designed a program called Frieze that could capture the image of a screen to a graphics file. He

4

sold the program through mail order, then moved to Atlanta, where he became a math professor at the Georgia Institute of Technology College of Management.

Working in his spare time, he created one of the first paint programs for the PC. He founded ZSoft in 1983 to market the new program, which he christened "PC Paintbrush."

Zachmann's young company got an early boost from two contracts with other PC vendors. Tecmar bundled PC Paintbrush with its color video adapters for the PC, and Microsoft bundled the software with its mouse. ZSoft's relationship with Microsoft continues to this day: the current version of PC Paintbrush is still bundled with the mouse, and Microsoft Windows includes a version of PC Paintbrush as one of the accessories sold with the program.

In the years that followed PC Paintbrush 1.0, ZSoft introduced regular upgrades to the software along with additional programs like Publisher's Paintbrush and Publisher's Type Foundry. The company's programs became increasingly popular, and ZSoft's PCX file format became a standard for storing paint graphics on the PC. PhotoFinish is thus the latest step in the software evolution that began with PC Paintbrush.

In 1992, ZSoft merged with WordStar International, a company that developed one of the first popular word processors for microcomputers. ZSoft, still based in Atlanta, is now known as the WordStar Advanced Technology Center. Zachmann remains as ZSoft's Chief Technical Officer.

Now that we know more about ZSoft, let's explore the functions and capabilities in PhotoFinish.

CHAPTER 1

The Basics of Color Imaging

Although PhotoFinish is capable of working with black-and-white or gray-scale images, its features are really oriented toward the manipulation of color photographs that have been captured, digitized, and stored on a microcomputer's hard disk. As such, PhotoFinish is part of a digital color revolution that has touched many industries involved in graphic communication, including publishing and photography.

Magazines, newspapers, and other publications are increasingly produced using relatively inexpensive microcomputer systems in conjunction with scanners, imagesetters, proofing devices, and other hardware. Eastman Kodak's Photo CD offers an inexpensive way to have snapshots stored in digital format on a compact disc, from which they can be imported into a computer system. Printing experts who once scoffed at the quality of digital images find themselves struggling to tell the difference between computer-generated pages and those produced by traditional means.

For most people, color is easy to take for granted. We may have to adjust the hue or brightness settings on our television sets every now and then, but for the most part, we don't give much thought to the way color is perceived—unless our favorite newscaster suddenly appears to be a shade of green. However, some knowledge of color perception is important if you want to get the most out of PhotoFinish and the other components in a color publishing system. Fortunately, PhotoFinish's Color

Picker function will make the concepts behind color perception easier to understand.

The Perception of Color

Color is, to put it simply, light. You've probably seen the experiments where a beam of light is shone through a prism and breaks apart into the colors of the rainbow. Each color represents a different frequency of light; when light of a certain frequency hits our eyes, we perceive it as the color corresponding to that frequency.

Color perception is such an integral part of our lives that it is easy to overlook the complexity of the process. Many factors affect the way we perceive color images or objects, including the level of surrounding light and the medium through which the image is presented.

Our perception of printed images can vary depending on the paper stock and inks used on press. Our perception of images displayed on a television set or computer monitor can vary depending on the age and make of the tube.

Transmissive and Reflective Color

In computer-based color imaging, we are interested in two kinds of color: reflective and transmissive. Reflective color is what we see most often in everyday life. When we look at an orange, for example, we see light reflected back from the fruit. The surface of the fruit absorbs all colors except orange, then reflects the remaining frequency (orange) back to the eye. If a surface absorbs all colors, it appears black. If it absorbs no colors, it appears white. (Figure 1-1)

Transmissive color is color emitted from a luminous source. It includes color generated by a television set or computer display. Instead of seeing color as reflected from a light-absorbing surface, we see it directly transmitted from a light source.

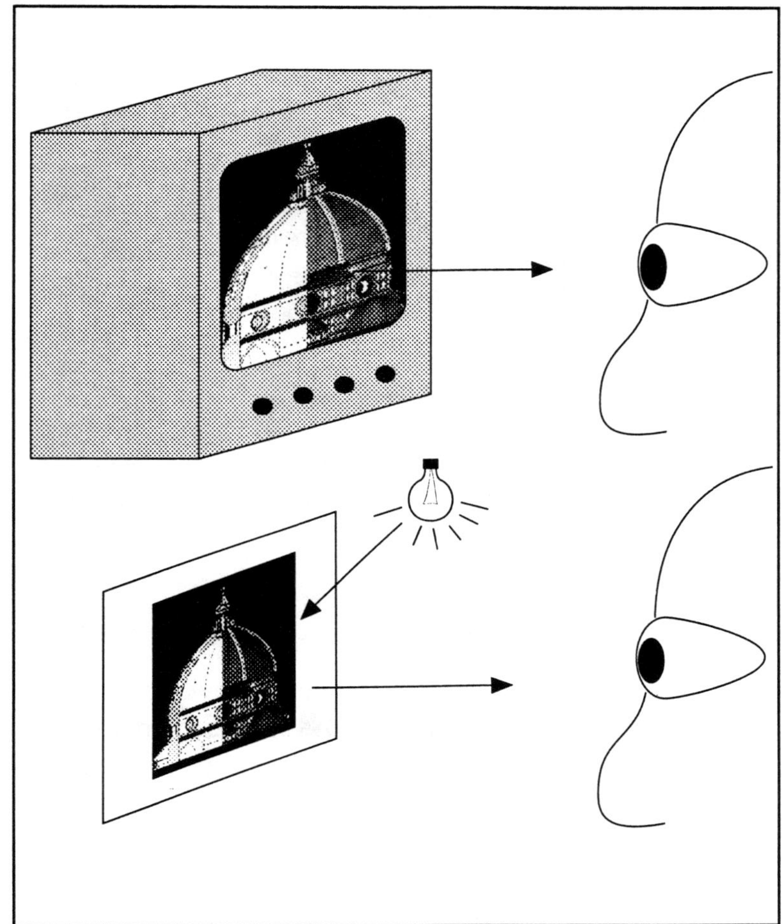

The distinction between transmissive and reflective color is important because programs like PhotoFinish need to deal with both. Computer monitors, by their nature, show images in the form of transmitted light. However, the processes used to print and reproduce pages are based on reflective colors. PhotoFinish is capable of handling images that can be displayed or printed. But as many color publishers have learned, printed images almost always look different from when they appeared on the computer screen. The skill in being a computer publisher is knowing how to compensate for these differences. Fortunately, PhotoFinish includes calibration tools that make this easier.

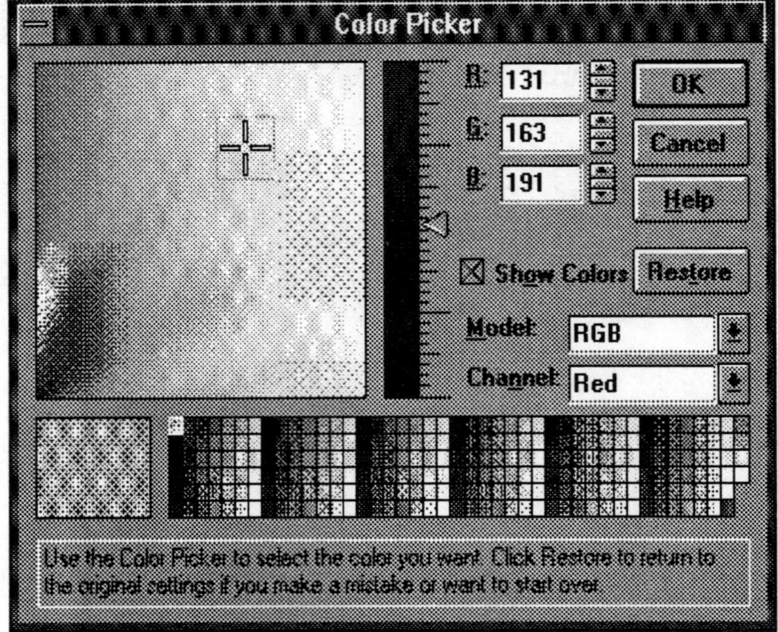

Color Models and Spaces

"Transmissive" and "reflective" are only general terms used to describe the way color is generated and perceived. To be more precise in their descriptions of color, imaging experts use what are known as "color models." In a color model, a color is described as a combination of certain "primary" colors or color components.

These colors are known as "primaries" because they are the building blocks of all other colors within their color model. (It should be noted that PhotoFinish uses the term "primary color" in a much different way, to describe the color currently being used to draw with.)

PhotoFinish supports three color models: RGB, CYMK, and HLS.

RGB: RGB, for Red, Green, and Blue, is the model used for color display in the television and computer industries. It is most often used as a way of describing transmissive color. In the RGB model, colors are described as being various combinations of red, green, or blue. If red, green, and blue are combined in equal percentages, they produce white. If they are absent, they produce black. RGB is also the color model used by most scanners and all computer displays. You can see how colors are formed in the RGB model by using the PhotoFinish Color Picker function. First, launch the program, go to the "File" menu, and choose "New" to create a new file. A "New File" dialog box comes up; don't bother with the settings at this point. Just click "OK."

Now go to the Options menu, then the Palette submenu, and select "Color Picker" (Figure 1-2). The Color Picker dialog box appears.

This dialog box allows you to replace any color in the PhotoFinish "Palette" with another. The currently selected color (the color you are changing) is seen in a corner of the dialog box. You can work in any of the three models, which you select from a "Model" list. Select "RGB" if it isn't selected already. The idea here is to create a color as a certain combination of Red, Green, and Blue.

We do this by choosing a value for each of the three primaries between 0 (no color) and 255 (maximum color). First, select Red as your "Channel," and move the slider control in the center of the dialog box to adjust the level of that color.

You can also enter a numeric value between 0 and 255. Then select Green and Blue and do the same thing. When you are finished, you will have created your own color as a certain combination of the three primaries. But don't close the dialog box just yet.

CYMK: CYMK, which stands for Cyan, Yellow, Magenta, and Black, is the color model used in the printing industry. Instead of being based on the transmissive colors red, green, and blue, it is based on reflective primaries, cyan (a light blue), yellow, magenta (a purplish red), and black.

Just as most colors can be displayed as RGB combinations on the screen, most colors can be reproduced as CYMK combinations on the page. When a color photograph is reproduced in print, the printing press generally uses four plates: one containing all cyan elements, one containing all yellow elements, and so on. In a four-color offset press, the plates are mounted in each of four printing stations that use inks in each of the process colors.

As a sheet of paper moves through the press, the stations apply the primary colors: cyan, then yellow, then magenta, then black (though not necessarily in that order). When the dots of process color inks are combined on the page, they create an illusion much like the original photograph. Theoretically, cyan, yellow, and magenta can be used to reproduce all printable colors, but in practice, they do a poor job of reproducing black and other dark shades. As a result, black is added to the CYM mix.

Using the same Color Picker dialog box, you can see how the RGB color you produced would be described as a CYM color (sans black). Just select "CYM" as your color model, and the RGB color you created will be shown as percentages of cyan, yellow, and magenta. Instead of choosing from Red, Green, and Blue channels, you can now select from Cyan, Yellow, and Magenta channels. The image itself won't change (unless you move the slider control), but the percentages of CYM will be different from the percentages of RGB. Keep in mind that PhotoFinish can only approximate how the image will look in CYM format. After all, the image is still being displayed on an RGB device. In general, an image on screen will appear to have brighter, more vibrant colors than the same image in print.

HLS: HLS, for Hue, Lightness, and Saturation, is different from the other color models in that it is based on properties other than color. In the HLS model, hue refers to the actual color, lightness refers to its brightness or darkness, and saturation refers to its purity.

Again, you can see the effects of various levels of hue, lightness, and saturation by experimenting with the color picker controls. When you select Hue as the Channel, you can choose a value from 0 to 360, with 0 or 360 representing red, 60 representing yellow, 120 representing green, 180 representing cyan, and so on. When you select Lightness or Saturation, you can adjust the settings from minimum (0) to maximum (1).

Color Publishing Systems

Before the Digital Era, color images were generally reproduced by one of two means: either through a printing process, such as offset lithography, or by a photographic process. In the photographic process, images are exposed one at a time on a silver halide plate.

In traditional offset lithography, an operator uses a proprietary color prepress system to produce color separations on film, which are converted to plates and placedonpress. Inexpensive microcomputers, in conjunction with peripheral devices like scanners and imagesetters, have created many new options for producing and reproducing color images.

These options range from digital color separations created on a PostScript imagesetter to 35 mm slides produced on film recorders and continuous-tone photographic prints produced on a dye-transfer printer. Microcomputers still have limitations as color production machines, but hardware and software developers have made enormous strides in improving the quality of their color publishing products.

"Experts" and so-called "dot doctors" used to scoff at the quality of color images produced from the desktop, but now even the most quality-conscious publishers have turned to microcomputers for color production.Most of the early color publishing products for microcomputers were aimed at Apple's Macintosh. But PC applications like PhotoFinish are quickly narrowing the gap with the Mac. Driven by the popularity of Microsoft Windows and the availability of powerful but inexpensive 386 and 486 computers, many color publishers are now turning to the PC.

How A PC Handles Color

Computers, as you probably know, handle information in the form of numbers. Even if what you see on the screen looks like the ceiling of the Sistine Chapel, it all boils down to numbers that describe the appearance of each dot in the display.

Many computer experts—self-styled and otherwise—are notorious for the technical jargon they throw around with seeming ease. One user has an "8-bit" display while another boasts of a "24-bit" display. One has just four megabytes of RAM while the other has 16. In some cases, this jargon serves little more than to intimidate the uninitiated.

However, the terms do mean something, and understanding them is important if you want to get the most out of packages like PhotoFinish. So let's spend a moment to discuss what happens inside a computer when it is running PhotoFinish.

Bits and Bytes

Most people use the Base 10 numbering scheme; that is, we count using a system of digits from 0 to 9. Computers, however, use a much simpler numbering scheme: Base 2, also known as the "binary" system. In Base 2, we count using only two digits, 0 and 1. The number "10" in Base 2 is actually "2" in Base 10. The number "8" in Base 10 is "1001" in Base 2. If you don't believe it, try counting:

Base 10	1	2	3	4	5	6	7	8
Base 2	0001	0010	0011	0100	0101	0111	1000	1001

Base 2 may seem like an inefficient way to count things. But it makes a lot of sense for computers, because 0 and 1 are easily represented by electronic signals. An "Off" signal corresponds to a "0," and an "On" signal corresponds to a "1."

This single piece of information—"0" or "1," "On" or "Off"—is known as a "bit," short for "binary digit." The bit is the basic building block of computer information. But because the bit can only describe a limited amount of information, it is grouped with other bits into a unit known as a "byte." A byte is a unit of information that consists of eight bits. Whereas a bit can be one of two values—0 or 1—a byte can be one of 256 possible values. That's how many numbers there are if you count from 00000000 to 11111111.

It turns out that 256 is a significant number in many ways. Given 256 possible values, you can store each character in the English language, along with many non-English characters and symbols. Thus we have ASCII, the American Standard Code for Information Interchange, the standard file format used for exchange of text documents and databases on personal computers.

ASCII assigns one of 256 codes to each letter, symbol, or number in the ASCII Character Set. Each character requires a byte of data, and as a result the number of characters in a text file corresponds to the number of bytes it consumes on a hard disk.

The number 256 is also significant in computer imaging. When the typical human eye perceives an image, it can distinguish no more than 256 different shades of a particular color. Thus a black-and-white photograph reproduced as a halftone in a newspaper needs to have only 256 shades of gray to look realistic.

Because the byte is a convenient measurement unit and also because 256 does such a nice job of describing pixels (picture elements), most scanners and displays use 8 bits as their basic

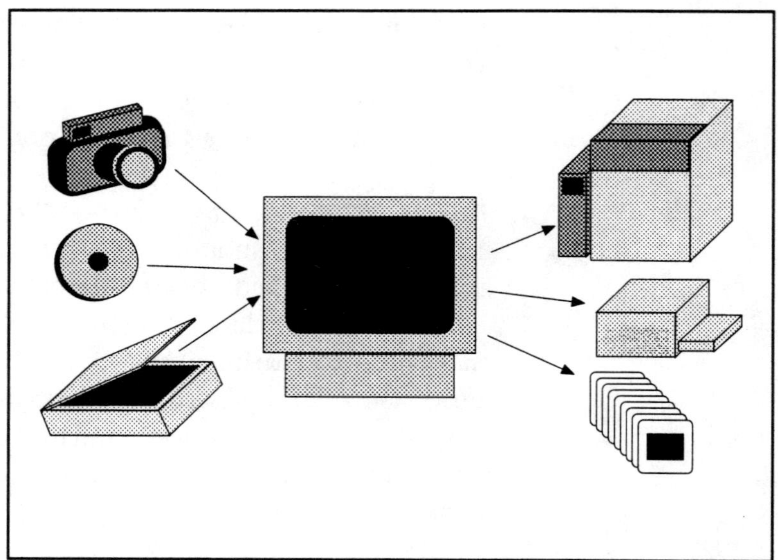

increment of image data. For example, most flatbed scanners used in gray-scale imaging are known as "8-bit" devices.

This means that the scanner can sense and transmit to the computer 8 bits of data—or one of 256 possible values—for each segment of the image scanned. An "8-bit" display can show up to 256 colors or gray shades for each dot on the screen. (They could just as easily be called "one-byte" scanners or displays, but this could imply that they were edible, we suppose.)

In color publishing, we multiply everything by three. Color scanners are often known as "24-bit" devices because they capture 8 bits each of red, green, and blue. And "photorealistic" color displays also have 24-bit capabilities, again because they can show 8 bits each of RGB. These products are capable are capturing or displaying more than 16 million colors (that's the number of possible values when you string together 24 bits).

These terms—"8 bit" and "24 bit"—refer to what's known as "pixel depth." Each dot, or pixel, in the image can be one of 256 values or one of 16.7 million values. Pixel depth, in combination with the resolution and size of the image, determine how many kilobytes or megabytes of disk space it will consume. The formula is this:

$$\text{File size} = \text{Pixel depth} \times \text{image size} \times \text{resolution}^2$$

Suppose you have a 2 x 3 inch image scanned at 100 dots per inch and 24 bits per pixel. There are 6 square inches and 10,000 (100 x 100) dots per square inch. That's a total of 60,000 dots. Since each dot consumes three bytes (24 bits) of data, we have a total of 180,000 bytes. Now we're in the realm of the kilobyte, which is equal to 1024 bytes, and the megabyte, equal to 1024 kilobytes. Some hard drives these days are actually measured in gigabytes, which are 1024 megabytes. The image described above would come in at about 176 kilobytes, but you could be forgiven for eyeballing it and saying "180K."

From Scan to Print

The typical color publishing system includes a scanner or other input device, a microcomputer workstation with a color monitor, and a digital color output device used for preliminary proofing (Figure 1-3). Another common "component" is a service bureau equipped with a PostScript imagesetter and a film-based proofing system. The digital prepress process works something like this:

The computer operator begins with color photographs, either prints or transparencies. These photographs are scanned using an appropriate scanner and scanning software and stored on disk. The function of the scanner is to convert light reflected from (or transmitted through) the original photograph into a series of bytes that can be stored in a computer file.

The scanner can be a flatbed model, used for scanning prints; a slide scanner, used for 35 mm slides; or a desktop drum scanner, which can scan slides, prints, or large-format transparencies. As an alternative to the scanner, the operator can import an image from a Photo CD disc or use a digital camera that store images directly in a computer-readable format.

Once the image is scanned, the operator then uses a program like PhotoFinish to retouch, color-correct, or otherwise modify the images. The corrected images are imported into a page layout program, such as Aldus PageMaker or QuarkXPress, where they are combined with text and other graphics.

Once the page layout is complete, the operator prints a preliminary proof on a laser printer or color printer. After any needed corrections or modifications are made, the job is stored on a high-capacity removable hard disk or optical disk and transported to a service bureau.

Employees at the service bureau use the customer's file to produce output on a PostScript imagesetter. PostScript is a page description language developed by a Mountain View, CA, company called Adobe Systems. Printers and other output devices equipped with PostScript have enhanced capabilities for producing text and graphics. PostScript imagesetters use the PostScript language to produce output on film or photographic paper. The more advanced models can produce color separations as negatives on film. We will discuss PostScript in greater detail in Chapter Nine.

In addition to the separations, the service bureau may also provide a film-based proof. These proofs, generated directly from the separations, are produced on expensive proofing systems from companies like 3M, Du Pont, Agfa, and Enco. The proofs provide a highly accurate—though not always perfect—representation of what the color image will look like in print. The separations and proofs are then taken to a commercial printer, who uses them to produce a color print job.

This is all a far cry from the proprietary systems that are still used to produce many color print jobs. These proprietary systems, sold by companies like Scitex, Crosfield, and Linotype-Hell, offer top-notch image quality, but also cost hundreds of thousands of dollars and are often limited by their inability to work with components from other manufacturers.

Digital prepress systems are relatively inexpensive, and can work with components from a variety of vendors. The downside is that the components don't always work together as smoothly as they should. Every scanner, display, and printer handles color a little differently, and each introduces its own bias as the image passes through the system. The calibration functions in PhotoFinish can go a long way toward correcting these inconsistencies, but users should still be aware of this challenge posed by digital color.

Hardware Requirements

The microcomputers used to capture and reproduce color images don't look all that much different from the first IBM PCs to adorn the desks of corporate America. But under the hood, these machines are a far cry from from those original PCs. We can see from the example above that color images consume a lot of data. That data must be stored, processed, displayed, and printed, and this calls for powerful hardware along the way.

PhotoFinish has a set of minimum and recommended hardware requirements. But if you want to get the most out of the program, more is better: more memory, more disk space, a more powerful processor. While the program works well on a 386 with 4 megabytes of RAM, you will soon find yourself wishing for more. The two most important specifications for working with color images are internal memory—RAM—and hard disk storage.

When you manipulate an image in PhotoFinish, it stores as much of the image as it can in RAM. The remaining portions of the image are stored on the hard disk and have to be called into memory as needed. Because accessing RAM is much faster than accessing data on a hard disk, PhotoFinish works best when you can fit all of an image into RAM. We recommend at least 8 megabytes of RAM, and if possible, 16. The nice thing about the extra RAM is that it allows you to be more productive even when you are not using PhotoFinish. For example, a lot of RAM makes it possible to launch several programs simultaneously, meaning that you can quickly switch between them. This is especially useful in desktop publishing applications, which generally involve interaction between several different types of software packages.

You need as much hard disk space as possible to accommodate the large file sizes of the color images you'll be manipulating with PhotoFinish. There is a version of Murphy's Law in computer graphics: no matter how large your hard disk, it will quickly fill up with software applications and the files they create. This is especially true if you plan to use multimedia applications with their video and sound files. A computer with 100 megabytes of disk storage was once considered excessive; now it's considered the bare minimum. In addition to your hard disk, it is a good idea to have a removable hard drive unit if you plan to work with a service bureau. Given the large size of color files, the 1.44-megabyte capacity of high-density diskettes won't do you much good. Most service bureaus use SyQuest-compatible removable drives, but check with your service bureau before buying one (more on working with your service bureau later).

Another essential component in a color publishing system is a display capable of showing photorealistic—that is, 24-bit—color. You can get by with a plain VGA display if you plan to work exclusively with gray-scale images, but a 24-bit display is highly recommended for working with color photographs. Otherwise, some images will appear to be dithered: the software will simulate colors outside the system palette using a pattern of dots. The problem is that you cannot be absolutely sure what effects your image modifications will have if you can't see a realistic display of the colors. Fortunately, 24-bit display boards can be acquired for less than $200. Some of the more expensive models ($500 to $1000) offer graphics acceleration features, which can be a blessing considering the amount of data these displays are expected to show. The greater the amount of data, the slower your display.

The question of processor performance is also important. A 386 equipped with sufficient memory and hard disk storage can do an excellent job of running PhotoFinish. But color image manipulation is a calculation-intensive process, and the more powerful your CPU, the better. In addition to the CPU and display, you will need some means of capturing and printing images. These hardware options are covered more thoroughly in later chapters. With its ability to retouch, enhance, and otherwise modify color images, PhotoFinish is an important element in a color publishing system. In the next chapter we will begin to explore its many features.

CHAPTER 2

Introduction to PhotoFinish

In Chapter One, we saw that personal computers have created a revolution in visual communication. Desktop computers are used to prepare page layouts for publication, to produce 35mm slides for business presentations, and even to create animations and interactive multimedia products. PhotoFinish is part of a software category that plays an important role in this revolution. This category is known by several names: photo editing software, image-editing software, image-processing software, and so on. Whatever you want to call them, these programs specialize in modifying color photographs and other images that have been converted into a digital format. But saying that they can "modify" a photograph is sort of like saying that Michelangelo "modified" the ceiling of the Sistine Chapel.

As we saw in Chapter One, a digital image is nothing more than a collection of numbers. What PhotoFinish provides is a broad array of tools that allow you to manipulate those numbers in mind-numbing ways.

Using PhotoFinish, you can scan a photographic image using a desktop scanner or video digitizer, enlarge or reduce it, brighten underexposed areas, darken overexposed areas, remove scratches, and then prepare the image for output on a printer or imagesetter. If an image has a reddish cast, you can reduce the level of red. Or green. Or blue. You can adjust the contrast to bring out otherwise hidden details.

You can even create illusions that look like reality: photos of your favorite movie stars with their arms around you, or a shot of your worst enemy dumping toxic waste into the city water supply.

Most of the tools and functions in PhotoFinish are similar to those found in other image-editing programs. The difference is that PhotoFinish offers these tools in an inexpensive and easy-to-use package. And it does have some features not found in some of its costlier rivals, including automated calibration functions, a moire removal function, photo retouch tools that incorporate image processing functions, and a Local Undo tool that selectively removes the effects of the previous operation. All of these functions will be described in the pages ahead.

In this chapter, we will provide a general introduction to PhotoFinish. We'll discuss the program's capabilities and limitations, and help you get set up to take full advantage of its features. In Chapter Three, we will provide an overview of the program's menu structure, and in Chapter Four we will look at its workboxes.

What PhotoFinish Can Do

PhotoFinish is a graphics program designed for use with bit-mapped images. Bit-mapped images, simply put, are images created from an array of dots, like miniature versions of the images we see on scoreboards at sporting events. They are also known as raster images.

In a sense, all images produced by computer systems are bit-mapped. Even the output of a laser printer is composed of tiny dots. Bit-mapped images are different from other kinds of computer-generated images in that the computer recognizes them and stores them as an array of dots.

The other major category of computer images consists of what are known as vector or draw graphics. A vector graphic appears on the computer screen as an array of dots. When printed on a laser printer, it also appears as an array of dots (at least when held to a magnifying glass). But inside the computer, the graphic is really a series of mathematical expressions. For example, imagine a stop sign. In a bit-mapped image, the stop sign is a series of dots arranged into an octagon. In a vector image, the stop sign would be a set of mathematical expressions that boil down to these instructions: go up four inches, take a 45-degree turn to the right, go another four inches, take another 45-degree turn, and so on.

The distinction between vector and bit-mapped graphics is important. PhotoFinish can work with most bit-mapped graphics, but it cannot work with vector graphics. Graphics packages that work with vector formats are known as "illustration" programs and include CorelDraw, Adobe Illustrator, Aldus FreeHand, and Micrografx Designer. Computer-assisted design (CAD) programs like AutoCAD also use vector graphics.

Vector graphics have several advantages over bit-mapped graphics. They are resolution-independent, meaning they can be printed at the full resolution of the output device. Print them on a laser printer, and they appear at 300 dpi (or whatever the resolution of the printer may be). Print them on an imagesetter, and they may appear at 1200 dpi or more. Bit-mapped graphics, on the other hand, are essentially locked at a fixed resolution. If you scan an image at 300 dpi and print it on a 2400-dpi imagesetter, it will still appear at its original resolution.

Another advantage of vector graphics is that they can be enlarged or reduced without loss of image quality. Bit-mapped graphics that are enlarged a great deal will soon appear to have a jagged quality. For this reason, vector formats are generally used to store and reproduce graphics that include text or must otherwise be reproduced at different sizes, such as corporate logos or trademarks (though bit-mapped images can also include text effects as well).

However, bit-mapped graphics also have their advantages.

Many kinds of images, including black-and-white and color photographs, can only be stored as bitmaps. Images captured by a scanner or digital camera are bit-mapped. In addition, bit-mapped images are generally easier to draw, modify, and manipulate.

Bit-Mapped Formats

Within the world of bit-mapped graphics, PhotoFinish can do a great deal. It can work with four kinds of images: black-and-white, gray-scale, 256-color, or 24-bit color.

Black-and-white images are also known as "single-bit" images because each dot requires just a single bit of information: it's either on (black) or off (white). They are the easiest to work with because they tend not to consume excessive memory resources. However, if you limit yourself to editing black-and-white images with PhotoFinish, you're wasting most of the program's features.

Gray-scale images, usually black-and-white scanned photographs, are those in which each dot can be one of 256 shades of gray. They are also known as 8-bit images for reasons that should be clear if you read the last chapter.

PhotoFinish provides many tools for working with gray-scale images. If you open a gray-scale image with less than 256 shades of gray, PhotoFinish automatically converts it to the 8-bit format.

Surprisingly enough, 256-color images are those consisting of 256 colors. In the last chapter, we noted that 256 was something of a magic number because it is roughly equal to the number of gray levels needed to make photographs look realistic.

Unfortunately, 256 is not so magic when it comes to color. In most cases, a palette of 256 colors is not capable of realistically reproducing photographs. To do that, you need 24-bit color, which is 256 times 256 times 256 (for something a little over 16.7 million).

To get a graphic demonstration of the difference between 8-bit and 24-bit color, try opening one of the sample images that came with the program (we're assuming here that you have a 24-bit display). Look at it in 24-bit mode, then convert it to 256 colors using the Convert option in the Image menu.

You will see that the smooth colors in the original have now been converted into a pattern of multi-colored dots. This is a process known as dithering, and it's the software's way of squeezing a huge color palette into a much smaller one.

However, 256-color images have their uses. If you want to create original artwork, you may find that a 256-color palette is well suited to your needs. Many images created by older paint programs may fall into this category.

If you have a choice in the matter, you'll find that 256-color images consume much less storage space than 24-bit images. Still, many of the image processing functions in PhotoFinish work with gray-scale and 24-bit images, but not with 8-bit color images.

Where PhotoFinish really shines is in its ability to handle 24-bit color images. Each dot in a 24-bit image, as we noted earlier, can be one of more than 16.7 million colors. That pixel depth makes it possible to display photographs with a high degree of realism.

It is important to note here the distinction between images as displayed and images as stored in the computer. No matter what the resolution or pixel depth of your display, PhotoFinish retains all of the original image data in the image file.

If you have an 8-bit VGA color display and open a 24-bit file, the program will display the file as best it can, selecting the 256 colors that most closely match the colors in the original file.

You will still be limited in your ability to see the effects of many image operations, but the file will retain all 24 bits of data.

File Formats

In recent years, software vendors have established several standard formats for storing graphic images. Some of these formats are oriented toward vector graphics, others toward bit-mapped graphics, still others toward both.

PhotoFinish supports a wide range of bit-mapped image formats. With most of the formats, PhotoFinish provides both read and write support. This means it can open files and save files in that format. With other formats, PhotoFinish is limited to opening or saving the file, but not both.

PCX. PCX is the file format developed by ZSoft during the infancy of PC graphics. Because of the popularity of ZSoft's paint programs, PCX became something of a standard among graphic file formats for the PC. As a result, it is supported by many desktop publishng and computer graphics programs on the PC. Early versions of PCX were limited to black-and-white images or those with a limited number of colors. However, PCX can now be used to store gray-scale and 24-bit color images.

Along with PhotoFinish, ZSoft includes a utility program called PCXHDR that allows you to view information about selected PCX files. To run it, minimize PhotoFinish (click on the down arrow in the upper-right corner of the window), select the PhotoFinish Group from the Program Manager Window menu, and double-click on PCXHDR. PCX is PhotoFinish's default format when you save a file for the first time. However, it is not as widely supported as the TIFF format in the PC environment, and is hardly supported at all on the Macintosh.

TIFF. TIFF, short for "Tagged Information File Format," has become the standard for storing gray-scale and color images in both the PC and Macintosh environments. It is widely supported by desktop publishing and computer graphics programs, and is especially preferred if you plan to use a color separation program.

TIFF, which was developed by Aldus Corp. in cooperation with other developers, has gone through several modifications since it was first introduced in the mid-1980s. Most programs create TIFF files in the current version 5, but PhotoFinish could have trouble with earlier versions of TIFF. ZSoft provides a utility program called TIFFDUMP that allows you to view information about TIFF files. It can be accessed in the same manner as PCXHDR.

PhotoFinish offers several options for compressing TIFF files. This can be useful given the large size of the files, which can quickly clog your hard disk. However, you have to be careful when using these options: if your image is to be opened by another program, the destination software may not be capable of reading the compressed format.

When saving a 24-bit or 8-bit image (either gray-scale or color), you have the option of doing so in a compressed format. The file is compressed using a method known as LZW. LZW is a "lossless" form of compression, meaning it does not sacrifice any data when compressing the file. It typically reduces file size about 50 percent. You can also compress black-and-white images using the Packbits format or CCITT formats. Packbits provides a greater level of compression. The CCITT option employs the same compression scheme used for facsimile transmission.

JPEG. JPEG, short for Joint Photographic Experts Group, is a standard format that has emerged in the computer industry for compression and decompression of color and gray-scale images. It differs from LZW in that it uses a "lossy" approach to compression. You can compress images at varying ratios, but at a loss of picture data. If you compress the image just a little, the loss of image data is barely noticeable. But if you compress it by a high ratio, say 20:1, picture quality may be noticeably degraded.

PhotoFinish offers four options for balancing the JPEG compression ratio with loss of image data: Minimum Loss, Low Loss,

Medium Loss, or High Loss. The higher the loss, the smaller the file size. You can also enter custom values to create your own compression ratio. You can bring the compressed image up on screen to see the effects of any data loss, but this won't necessarily indicate how the image will look in print. Always keep a copy of the original image handy until you are confident that you are not sacrificing too much image data.

EPS. EPS, short for Encapsulated PostScript, is a file format capable of handling both bit-mapped and vector-based images. It is based on PostScript, the page description language developed by Adobe Systems. PostScript is a programming language that uses English-like commands to describe the creation of pages that can include text and graphics. Most computer graphics programs have the ability to produce PostScript files.

EPS is a special version of PostScript intended to allow exchange of graphic images among different programs and operating systems. The format includes the PostScript commands along with an image "header"—that is, a bit-mapped rendition of the image described by the program. EPS files can be printed on a PostScript laser printer or imagesetter, and can also be imported into many graphics programs. PhotoFinish can create EPS files, but it cannot open them. In most cases, EPS is not the preferred format for storing images. All color images tend to consume large amounts of file space, but EPS files are especially large. In addition, bit-mapped images stored in EPS format are pretty much locked in and cannot be modified, except for simple resizing or cropping functions. Another disadvantage is that documents that incorporate EPS files cannot be printed on a non-PostScript printer.

On the other hand, EPS files can come in handy if you want to produce output at a service bureau that does not have PhotoFinish—or even a PC—installed. You just save your image as an EPS file, copy it to a disk, and take it to the service bureau. There, the file can be printed directly on any PostScript printer or imagesetter.

INTRODUCTION TO PHOTO FINISH

Other formats. Other formats supported by PhotoFinish include BMP, GIF, MSP, and Targa.

BMP is the standard bit-mapped format used in Microsoft Windows. One reason to save an image in BMP format is if you wanted to use it as "wallpaper"—that is, a background for the Windows screen. BMP is also supported in the OS/2 operating system.

MSP is a format used by older versions of Microsoft Paintbrush. PhotoFinish can read MSP files, but cannot save them.

GIF is the format created by CompuServe for storing bit-mapped images intended for transmission over phone lines.

The Targa format, developed by TrueVision, was one of the first file formats capable of storing 24-bit color.

Clipboard. In addition to opening files saved in standard file formats, PhotoFinish allows you to open images that have been copied to the Windows Clipboard.

The Clipboard is a standard feature in Microsoft Windows that allows exchange of data—including graphics—among different files or even different programs. All Windows programs include functions that allow you to Cut or Copy selected text or graphics to the Clipboard. Once this is done, you can insert the same text or graphics into another document using the Paste command.

You can also capture an image of the screen using the PrtSc button, or an image of the current window using Alt-PrtSc. The image is copied to the Clipboard, from which it can be pasted into other documents.

Like other Windows applications, PhotoFinish allows you to import items from the Clipboard using the Paste command, which is found in the Edit menu (along with Cut and Copy). However, you can also open the contents of the Clipboard

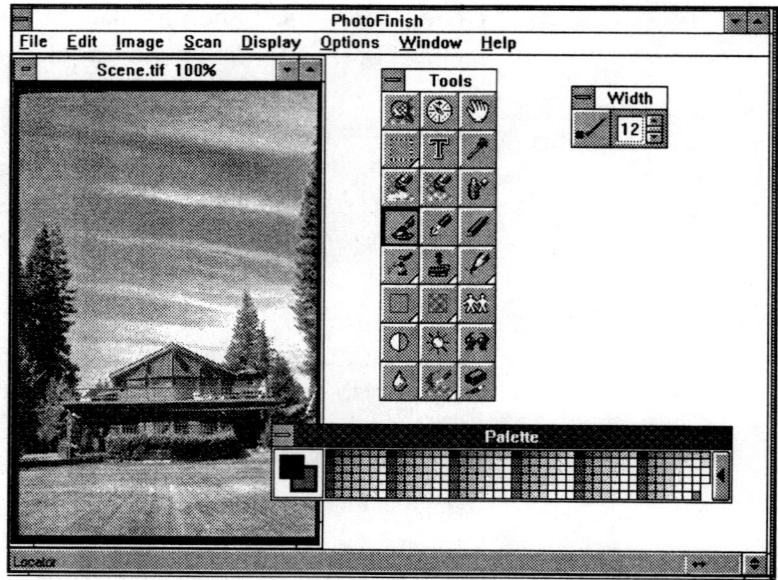

using the Open command from the File menu. Instead of choosing a file from the file list in the File Open dialog box, just click on the Clipboard button in the lower right-hand corner. Any image copied to the Clipboard is then placed into a new untitled file.

The screen displays you see in this book were created in this very manner. The nice thing about the Clipboard function is that it saves time. You can avoid creating a "New" file before you import the image that has been copied to the Clipboard. Better yet, when you open the image copied to the Clipboard, your file is automatically set at the proper size and with the correct number of colors. You don't have to bother with creating a new file with the proper dimensions.

The PhotoFinish Display

PhotoFinish provides access to its tools and features through pull-down menus and a series of "workboxes" that appear on the screen. The PhotoFinish display is one aspect of the program that got an extensive facelift in the move from version 2.0 to version 3.0.

INTRODUCTION TO PHOTO FINISH

Figure 2-2. Version 3.0 of PhotoFinish does away with the Width and Shape workbox, but adds a Ribbon bar that provides easy access to common functions. Version 3.0 also adds an AutoBar (not shown) that allows you to modify the effects of the tools.

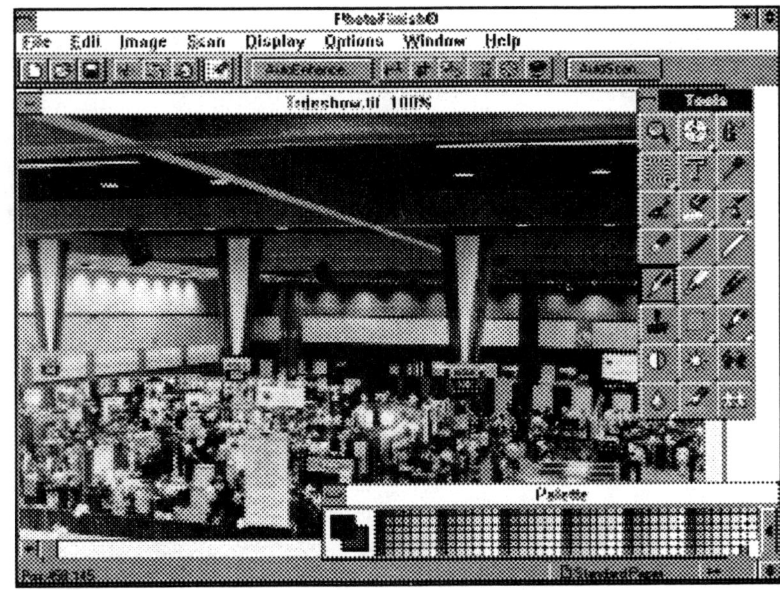

In version 2.0, the display consisted of a Palette, a Toolbox, and the Width and Shape box (Figure 2-1). Version 3.0 (Figure 2-2) does away with the Width and Shape box, incorporating its functions into new dialog boxes that allow you to modify the effects of the program's tools.

Version 3.0 also added two new elements to the display: a "Ribbon Bar" along the top of the screen that provides easy access to common functions, and an "AutoBar" that allows you to modify the effects of the currently selected tool without resorting to menu selections. The Ribbon Bar and AutoBar do not add any new functions to PhotoFinish; they merely make it easier to get to the functions already present in the program.

The Toolbox, along with the Image menu, provides the heart of the program's features. It includes tools for retouching and selecting areas of the image. Many of these tools were designed to simulate tools used in traditional art studios, such as charcoal and pencil. The Image menu, as we shall see in Chapter Three, includes a wide range of functions for adjusting and transforming images.

In traditional art, a palette is a board on which the artist can mix the paints to be used for a piece of art. The PhotoFinish Palette is an electronic version of the artist's palette. As a default, the Palette provides access to the colors or gray shades available for your image. If you are working in 24-bit mode, the palette includes 256 colors that you can select from the total palette of more than 16 million. If you are working in 256-color or gray-scale mode, the palette shows all the colors or gray shades that are available. (Remember that even if your display is capable of showing just 256 colors, PhotoFinish still lets you edit 24-bit images.)

On the left side of the Palette is the Color Selection box are two boxes, one partially covering the other. These boxes show the currently selected foreground and background colors used for painting operations.

Some PhotoFinish tools do not use the colors or gray shades in the default palette. For example, the Brightness tool allows you to make portions of an image darker or lighter. When this tool is selected, the Palette becomes a slider control that allows you to modify the degree to which the image will be lightened or darkened. In version 2.0, the Charcoal tool brings up a palette that allows you to choose from a series of gray shades. In version 3.0, however, you select the level of gray from within a dialog box. These functions will be described more extensively in Chapter Four.

When you open an existing image or create a new one, it appears in a window known as the Picture Window. You can have up to eight Picture Windows open at any one time, but only one can be the active window—meaning the one affected by image processing operations. Each Picture Window conforms to the standard Microsoft Windows controls. If an image is too large to fit within the window, you can scroll around using the scroll bars. You can also enlarge or reduce the window by dragging in the lower right-hand corner. The program's handling of windows will be discussed in greater detail in the next chapter.

At the bottom of the screen, a status bar provides information about the tool or function selected. It can also show the cursor's position or information about the position of the selected tool. When you select the Eyedropper tool, it shows you values corresponding to the color of the area over which the tool is positioned.

Optimizing Performance

One challenge of working with color images is the sheer amount of data needed to describe them. This not only affects your hard disk storage, but also the overall performance of the system. If your system lacks the horsepower needed to handle color images, you will find that even the simplest operations slow to a glacial pace.

The key specification that determines your system's ability to handle color is the amount of random-access memory (RAM). The minimum RAM requirement for Windows is 2 megabytes, but many users consider 4 megabytes to be the minimum practical requirement. If you are using PhotoFinish and you want to work with larger-than-wallet-sized images—without going insane, that is—you may need 8 or even 16 megabytes of RAM.

Here's why you need so much memory. When PhotoFinish works with an image, it stores as much of that image as it can in RAM. While residing in RAM, that image has to share space with portions of the operating system, the Windows environment, and the PhotoFinish software.

If the available memory can accommodate the image along with everything else, performance is relatively fast. However, if the software and image cannot entirely fit into RAM, PhotoFinish uses a technique known as "virtual memory" to simulate the extra memory.

Virtual memory uses a section of your hard disk to store software and data that would otherwise be stored in RAM. It is a nice feature because it allows your system to work with images that would otherwise be too big. However, that extra memory comes at a price. Accessing data on a hard disk takes much more time than accessing it in RAM.

The bottom line is that without sufficient RAM, you'll be watching the light on your hard disk flash away as you wait for even the most rudimentary image processing operations to be completed.

The best solution to this problem is to get more RAM. The next best solution is to work around the limitations of your system.

One strategy is to maximize the amount of RAM available to your system. Any open files, windows, or programs that are not essential should be closed; even a window that has been minimized consumes some memory. Turn off any memory-resident programs, even useful ones like Adobe Type Manager. Look at the video driver (a piece of software that provides compatibility with your monitor) to see if it is consuming any extra memory.

Some video boards offer you the option of reserving part of RAM to speed up the graphic display; turning this feature off will likely speed up any operations that do not involve redrawing the screen.

Another strategy is to work with images that fit within your computer system's memory limitations. In Chapter Five, we'll discuss resolution options for scanning images. You'll find that you don't always need to scan at the highest possible resolution to get the best-looking image. By keeping image resolution as low as possible—without sacrificing quality—you can reduce the amount of data needed to store the image.

Likewise, limiting the physical size of the image can also limit its file size. When scanning an image, crop it as closely as possible to what you'll ultimately need. And don't scan

an image at a full 8-inch width if it is going to be reduced
to two inches in print.

Now that we've covered the basics, we're ready to move on to
looking at the features in PhotoFinish. In the next two chapters,
we will explore the many functions and tools found in
PhotoFinish.

C HAPTER 3

PhotoFinish Menus

Most of the functions in PhotoFinish are found in two places: either through pull-down menus at the top of the screen, or from a moveable toolbox that first appears to the right of the screen.

In this chapter, we will provide an overview of the PhotoFinish menu structure. It is not meant to be an exhaustive description of all features; for this you can refer to the user manual. Instead, we will offer a map to the program's key functions, many of which will be explored further in later chapters. In Chapter Four, we will explore the PhotoFinish workboxes, including the Toolbox and Palette.

The PhotoFinish menu structure is one aspect of the program that did not change very much in the upgrade from version 2.0 to version 3.0. The Display menu, which controls what you see in the PhotoFinish display, has some minor changes that reflect the new screen layout options. The Image menu includes new Samples options and and two new effects: Apply Paper and Crumple. Otherwise, there is no difference between the two versions.

The pull-down menus in PhotoFinish work in a similar manner to those found in other Windows applications. If a menu item is followed by an ellipsis (…) that means it will bring up a dialog box if it is selected. Menu items followed by an arrow bring up a submenu.

Many functions found in the menus can also be accessed through keyboard shortcuts. Once you get to know them, you can use the shortcuts for speedier access to the functions. For example, holding down the Control key and hitting "S" has the same effect as selecting "Save" from the File menu. These shortcuts are identified next to the respective menu items.

The menus to the left of the screen will be familiar to any experienced Windows user: "File" includes options for opening, saving, viewing, and printing files. It also provides access to the PhotoFinish Printer Calibration function. The "Edit" menu includes the standard Windows commands for cutting, copying, pasting, and deleting selections, along with a few other options that will be discussed below.

The Window and Help menus that appear on the right of the screen will also look familiar. The Window menu controls the appearance (or disappearance) of windows on the screen, and offers a quick way to get from one window to another. The Help menu provides access to the PhotoFinish on-line Help system, which provides quick information on the program's functions. Help is also available from within most dialog boxes.

Next to the Edit menu is the Image menu, which provides much of the real power of PhotoFinish. This is where you will turn to automatically enhance images or produce one of many special effects. The Image menu also provides options for resizing and rotating images.

The Scan menu includes commands for capturing images with a scanner or video digitizer, along with scanner calibration functions. However, if you use the TWAIN interface to capture an image, the scanning options are accessed from the Acquire command that appears in the File menu (this command will not appear unless you choose to add the TWAIN interface).

The Display menu offers options for zooming in and out of an

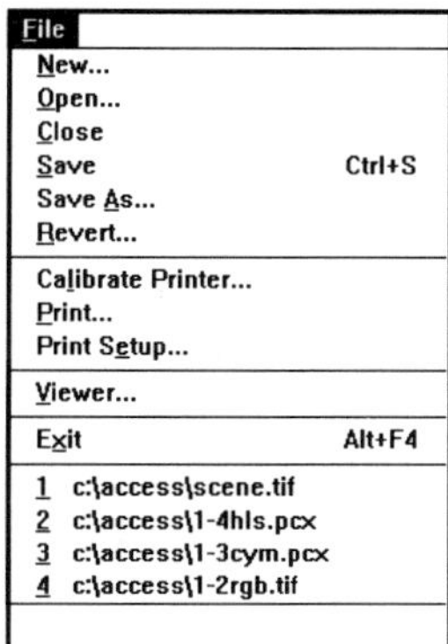

Figure 3-1. The File menu in PhotoFinish is similar to the File menus in other Windows applications.

image, controlling the screen layout (toolboxes and palettes), and calibrating the monitor.

The Options menu allows you to modify paintbrushes, palettes, color patterns, and other program elements. It also allows you to select typefaces for use with the Text tool. Now we'll look at some of these menus in greater detail. The Scan menu will be covered in detail in Chapter Five, which discusses scanning.

Because most of the options in the Options menu are used to control the Toolbox and Palette, they will be discussed in Chapter Four.

File Menu

The File menu in PhotoFinish (Figure 3-1) is not much different from the File menus in other Windows applications. Here is where you can open, close, save, or print files, or create a new one from scratch.

The PhotoFinish File menu also offers a Print Calibration function to accompany the Print command, along with a useful Viewer function that allows you to look at thumbnail versions of images before you import them. If you choose to add a TWAIN-compatible scanner or digitizer, the File menu also provides access to image-capture functions.

Figure 3-2. This dialog box appears when you select New from the File menu. The larger the width and height of the image, the more file space it will consume and the more memory you will need.

New

After you launch PhotoFinish, your first operation will generally be to open an existing file or create a new one. If you select the File New option, PhotoFinish presents a dialog box asking for the desired dimensions of the image and whether you want it to be black-and-white, gray-scale, 256-color, or 24-bit color (Figure 3-2). At the bottom of the dialog box is a line that informs you of how much memory the image requires and how much memory is available. The available memory includes virtual memory, which we described in the previous chapter. You can turn off the virtual memory feature using the Preferences selection under the Options menu. This will limit the size of the files you can work with. Keep in mind that the file size of the image is determined by its physical dimensions as well as the number of colors. These dimensions can be set in terms of the total number of dots in the image (pixels), or as a measurement in inches, centimeters, points, or picas. An inch equals 72 points or six picas.

Open/Close

The Open command provides access to the File Open dialog box. You can open up to eight existing files, but keep in mind that each open file consumes memory, so don't go overboard. You can also open files using the Viewer function (see below), but File Open is quicker.

The Close command is used to close a file; if you try to close a file without first saving it, PhotoFinish asks if you're sure you want to close it. If you close a file without saving it, you will lose any changes you have made since the last Save. Double-clicking on the small horizontal bar in the upper-left corner of the window has the same effect as selecting the Close command.

Save/Save As

The Save and Save As commands are used to store images in a file on disk. If you are working with a new, untitled file, the Save and Save As commands both bring up the Save As dialog box (Figure 3-3). This dialog box allows you to enter a name

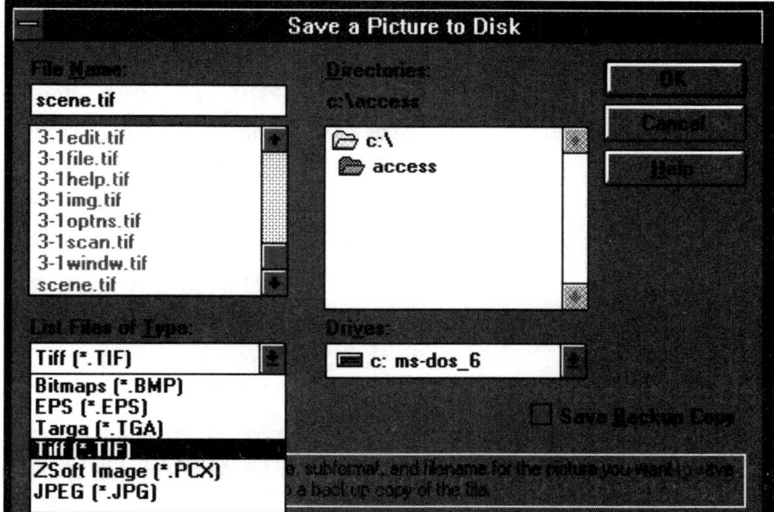

Figure 3-3. The Save As dialog box allows you to save files in one of several common graphics formats, such as TIFF. The correct file extension (.TIF) is automatically added when you select the file type.

and file type for the file. If you are working with an existing file, Save saves any changes you have made to the original file. Save As gives you the option of saving the file under a different name or file format.

Use the Save and Save As commands with caution if you have opened multiple windows of the same file. PhotoFinish allows you to open the same file multiple times; each time you open it, it is displayed in a new Picture Window. You can perform different, independent operations on each of the windows. However, if you use the Save command, only the currently active window will be saved under the original file name. If you want to save each version of the image, select each window in turn and choose the Save As command for each, saving them under different names.

In general, it is a good idea to save your work frequently. If you have an unforeseen power outage or your computer crashes, you will probably lose any work performed since the last time you saved the file.

You can also use the Save command as a form of error recovery. The Revert command (described below) abandons the current file and replaces it with the version that you last saved to disk.

As you are working on an image, save it whenever you reach a point where you are satisfied with your work. If you find that you have screwed up your artwork beyond even the ability of the Undo command to fix things, just go to the Revert option to bring up the last-saved version.

If you are performing extensive modifications on an image, it is a good idea to use the Save As option to save your work under a new file name. That way, you can go back to the original if you don't like the modifications.

Although the Save As dialog box appears to be simple, it provides access to one of the most powerful functions in PhotoFinish: the program's ability to support a wide range of file formats. You select these from a Format list that appears near the bottom of the dialog box.

For certain image formats, PhotoFinish offers additional options for compressing the file. These options are found in a File Sub-Format list that appears in the Save As dialog box. When saving a 24-bit or 8-bit TIFF image (either gray-scale or color), you can have the file compressed using the LZW method.

LZW is a "lossless" form of compression, meaning it does not sacrifice any data when compressing the file. It typically reduces file size about 50 percent. To decompress a TIFF image that has been saved in LZW format, you just open it through the PhotoFinish File Open dialog box and save it again in an uncompressed format. You can also choose from different compression ratios for the JPEG format. Remember that JPEG is a lossy compression scheme: the more you reduce the image's file size, the more image data you lose. PhotoFinish offers four JPEG options: Minimum Loss, Low Loss, Medium Loss, or High Loss. The higher the loss, the smaller the file size.

You can also enter custom values by choosing Custom Compression as the JPEG sub-format. The PhotoFinish manual tells you how to do this.

PHOTOFINISH MENUS

Whatever you do, it is a good idea to experiment before setting on a particular JPEG compression ratio. You can bring up the compressed image on screen to see the effects of any data loss, but this won't necessarily indicate how the image will look when it's in print. Always keep a copy of the original image handy until you are confident that you are not sacrificing too much image data.

Revert

The Revert option, as noted above, is a handy way to recover from errors that cannot otherwise be corrected using the Undo function. Revert closes the current file without saving it, then opens the previously saved version.

Any changes made to the file since you last saved it are lost. Because you could be losing some valuable work, Revert prompts you to make sure you really want to go back to the previous file.

Print

 The Print option is used to print your PhotoFinish documents on the selected printer. It is accompanied by a Print Calibration function, which makes adjustments to images so they will look as good as possible when printed on a particular output device. We will discuss printing from PhotoFinish in Chapter Nine.

Viewer

This option provides a handy way to view images before you open them. Given the eight-character file name limit in DOS, it is easy to give your graphics files cryptic names that may be easy to forget later on. With the Viewer option, you can get a rough idea of the file's contents. When you choose this option, thumbnail versions of the images on a particular drive or directory are displayed. You can change the drive or directory using the standard Windows Drives and Directories lists. When the Viewer function displays an image for the first time, it builds a low-resolution thumbnail version for display purposes. As a result, the thumbnails appear slowly on the screen, and the process can be painfully slow if there are a lot of images to be displayed. Once the thumbnail has been built, it displays much faster on subsequent views.

In the Preferences dialog box (found in the Options menu), you can choose to have thumbnails automatically created each time you save a file. Just select the Save Thumbnail Files option. Once files are displayed in the Viewer, you can open them, view information about them, move them to another directory, or delete or rename them.

Edit Menu

The PhotoFinish "Edit" menu, like the File menu, is similar to the Edit menus found in other Windows graphics programs. It includes standard commands for cutting, copying, pasting, and deleting selections, along with other options (Figure 3-4).

Undo

Undo is one of the truly great inventions of software developers. It recognizes the glorious imperfection of humanity: our tendency, every now and then, to do something that we would just as soon take back. Undo, true to its name, Undoes the last operation, restoring the image to what it looked like before you committed your blunder. It undoes everything you have done since you last selected your current tool or executed your last command.

This means that if you splatter your image with brown paint, then attempt to fix it with the eraser, Undo will restore anything you did with the eraser, but won't touch the paint. This is where the Revert command (File menu) comes in handy.

Cut, Copy, Paste

The Cut, Copy, and Paste commands allow PhotoFinish to interact with the Windows Clipboard. As we described above, the Clipboard is an electronic storage area for temporary placement of text or graphics. Images in PhotoFinish are placed on the Clipboard using the Cut or Copy commands.

Once they are placed on the Clipboard, they can be pasted into other PhotoFinish documents or into documents created with other programs. First, you select a portion of the image using the PhotoFinish selection tools (which are described later). Then, select either Cut or Copy to place the selected portion on the Clipboard. Cut deletes the selected portion from the current screen, while Copy retains the selected portion. The Delete option, found below the Paste option, deletes the selected portion without copying it to the Clipboard. If no portion of the image is currently selected, the Cut and Copy options will be grayed out on the menu (meaning they are not available). Likewise, if the Clipboard is currently empty, the Paste option will be grayed out.

Selection Commands

Most of PhotoFinish's functions for selecting portions of an image are found in the Toolbox. But the Edit menu does provide some limited selection functions. These are found in the Select submenu at the bottom of the menu: Select All, Select None, Leave Original, and Transparent.

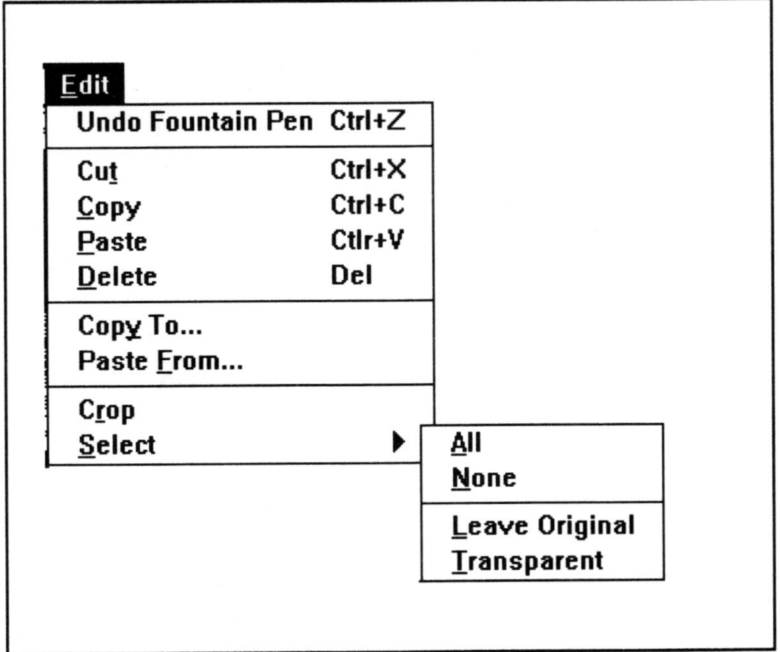

Figure 3-4. The PhotoFinish "Edit" menu includes standard commands for cutting, copying, pasting, and deleting selections, along with a few other options

Select All. The Select All option provides a quick way to select the entire image, which can then be cut or copied to the Clipboard. Just choose Select All and you will see a dotted line (known as a selection marquee) surrounding the image.

Select None. The Select None option cancels the current selection. It is most useful in conjunction with the selection tools, which are described in Chapter Four. The Leave Original and Crop options also work in conjunction with the selection tools found in the toolbox.

Copy To/Paste From. The Copy To and Paste From commands are extensions of the Copy and Paste commands. Instead of copying selected images to the Clipboard, you can copy them to a file.

This is handy if you want to break a large image file into smaller sections, or if you want to create a composite image by cutting and pasting, but do not want to tie up the Clipboard. It's sort of like having an unlimited number of Clipboards. You have the same options for saving the files as you do under the File Save dialog box. The Paste From command allows users to paste a stored image file into the current document.

Image Menu

The Image Menu (Figure 3-5) is where you find much of the power of PhotoFinish. It includes a wide range of commands for enhancing and transforming images. Some of the commands are aimed at improving the overall appearance of the image and making it look as close to the original as possible. Others are aimed at producing special effects and other transformations that make the image look unrecognizable.

The Image menu has five major submenus: Filter, Special Effect, Tune, Convert to, and Transform. You can also apply automatic image enhancement, change the resolution of an image, and call up information about an image.

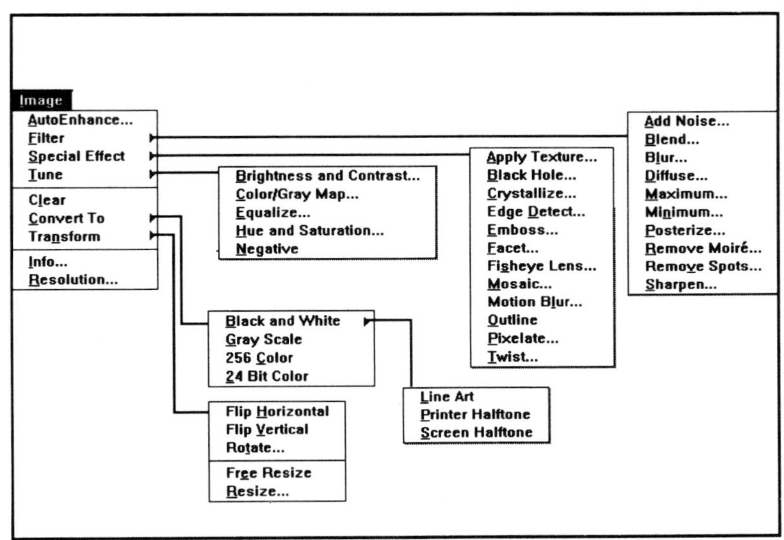

Automatic Image Enhancement is an especially powerful function that can provide basic modifications to an image with a single command. We will begin with a dicussion of this feature, then we'll move into the Image menu's other functions.

Automatic Image Enhancement

One of the primary functions of PhotoFinish is as an image correction tool. Most scanned images, especially when scanned on a relatively old scanner, are distorted in some way from the original.

One common problem is that midtones—the areas of gray or color between the darkest and lightest extremes—often are scanned darker than they should be. Or the image can be slightly crooked from its placement on the scanner's platen.

Another problem arises when you attempt to scan a halftone out of a newspaper or magazine. When you scan a halftone, it comes in as a screened image consisting of an array of dots. When the image is ultimately printed on a laser printer or imagesetter, it will be screened again.

The result, in most cases is a moire pattern: an unsightly grid that lays on top of the printed image. It is created by superimposing one screen on top of another (you can see a similar effect if you hold one window screen on top of another).

The scanner calibration functions in PhotoFinish provide one way to correct distortions during the scanning process. These functions will be described more extensively in the chapter on scanning.

However, the calibration functions are designed to correct scanning inaccuracies that show up consistently with a particular scanner. They do you little good if the image is too dark to begin with, or if the user happens to nudge the image out of alignment when it is placed in the scanner.

AutoEnhance can provide a set of default image modifications, or you can choose to customize the modification. The default modifications are: crop, straighten, adjust brightness, and adjust contrast.

If you want to customize the enhancement, you can also choose to have PhotoFinish apply automatic moire removal or saturation adjustment.

Moire removal removes the dot pattern from a scanned image, and is also available as a separate filter. Saturation adjustment automatically modifies the intensity of the colors to make them look more vibrant or more "washed out." Again, you can independently and manually adjust saturation using the Hue/Saturation command under the Tune submenu.

Any changes made to an image using AutoEnhance can be seen in a preview box. You can cancel the changes by clicking on the Cancel button in the dialog box or by selecting Undo after you have closed the dialog box.

In version 3.0, AutoEnhance is available from the Ribbon bar in addition to the Image menu. It could be that AutoEnhance provides the only modifications you need to make to the image.

But if you want to go further, you can turn to the options in the Image submenus: Filter, Tune, and Special Effects.

Filter

An image filter is a small program that modifies the pixels in an image to produce some sort of effect. As we saw in Chapter One, a digital image is nothing more than a collection of numbers. A filter changes the values of those numbers in a way that produces the desired modification. For example, the Sharpen filter sharpens the detail in the picture by changing the values of pixels on the borders of objects.

In some image-editing programs, the term "filter" is used to describe almost any function that provides a wholesale transformation of the image. However, PhotoFinish groups its image modification functions into three categories: Filter, Tune, and Special Effects.

The "Filter" filters, so to speak, consist mostly of the standard filters found in other image editing programs: Blur, Sharpen, Add Noise, and so on. These provide relatively modest modifications to the image. The Special Effects filters are aimed at more spectacular transformations. The Motion Blur effect, for example, modifies the image to look as if the subject was moving when the shot was taken.

The Tune filters are aimed at improving the general appearance of images by increasing or decreasing brightness, contrast, and other settings.

The filters found in the Filter submenu include Add Noise, Blend, Blur, Diffuse, Maximum, Minimum, Posterize, Remove Moire, Remove Spots, and Sharpen. Some of these filters can be customized by entering values in a dialog box, but others offer no customization options. The Diffuse filter works with any gray-scale or color image. The Remove Spots filter works with any color image. The other filters work only with gray-scale and 24-bit color images.

Any PhotoFinish filter can be applied to the entire image or to a portion of the image that has been selected using the selection tools.

If none of the image has been selected, the operation applies to the entire picture. Selection tools are discussed in greater detail in Chapter Four.

One major difference between PhotoFinish 2.0 and PhotoFinish 3.0 is the way they apply filters. When you choose a filter in PhotoFinish 2.0, a simple dialog box appears that allows you to modify the effects of the filter by choosing from several options or a "custom" option. preview their effect before actually applying them to the image. Do this by clicking on the Preview option in the dialog box for that filter. The image in the active picture window then appears as it would if the filter were applied.

In PhotoFinish 3.0, selecting a filter brings up a large dialog box presenting thumbnail samples of each option. Instead of previewing the option, you simply select the thumbnail image you want. By clicking on an "Advanced" button in the dialog box, you can enter custom values for the image effects.

Version 3.0 also includes a handy new "Samples" option (Figure 3-6) that allows you to quickly see the effects of all filters. It presents thumbnail versions of the current image as if it would look if the filter were applied. You can apply the filter or effect by double-clicking on the thumbnail. The Samples options is available in the Filters, Special Effects, and Tune submenus.

If you apply a filter by mistake (or find that it did not have the intended effect), you can go back to the original using the Undo command. This allows a great deal of freedom in experimenting with filters and other image processing tools. Considering that you can customize most of these filters and combine the effects of several filters on a single image, the possibilities for manipulating images are nearly infinite.

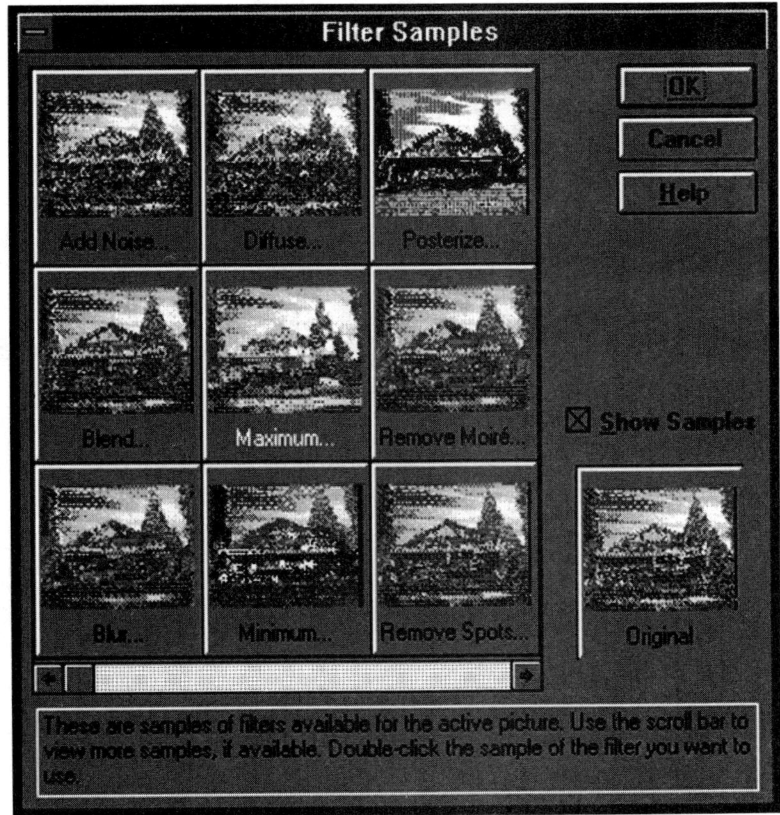

Add Noise

This filter creates a grainy, static-like effect by adding random dots to the image. It is sort of like watching the image on a television set with poor reception. In most cases, you would not do this to enhance the look of the image, but to create a special effect (Figure 3-7).

There are three preset levels of Add Noise—Light, Medium, and Heavy—plus a customize option that allows you to set your own level. The customize option allows you to select the amount of noise to add using values from 0 (none) to 255 (maximum).

You can also choose a Distribution option—Bell curve or Flat—which determines which pixels in the image are affected

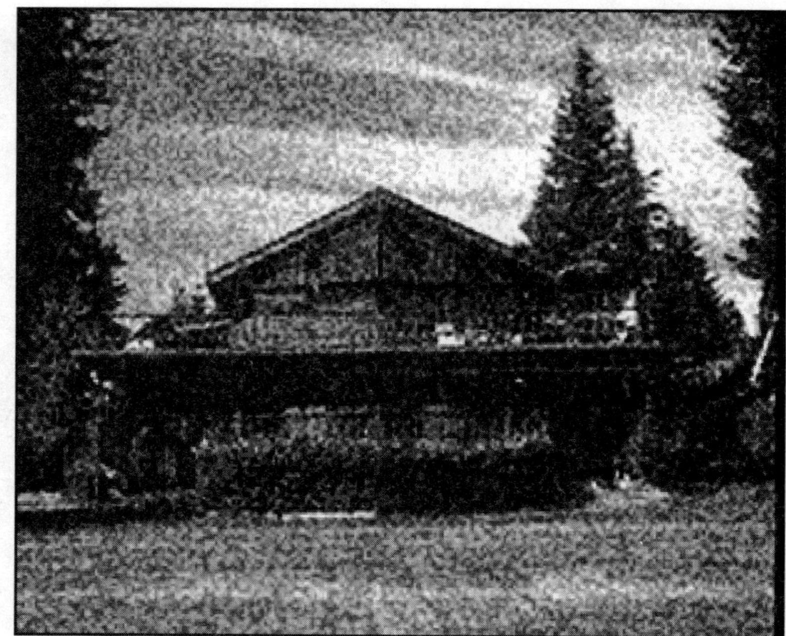

by the filter. A Flat distribution, which affects all pixels equally, works the fastest and creates the most pronounced changes. Finally, you can apply the filter to selected channels—Red, Green, or Blue—or apply it to all colors equally.

Blend

This filter (Figure 3-8) is used to soften and smooth the colors in an image. It is similar to the "Soften" filter found in other image editing programs. If an image appears to have too much contrast between neighboring dark and light areas, this filter will blend the areas together, making the transition smoother. Again, you can choose from Light, Medium, or Heavy application of the effect. You can also customize the blend by adding a value between 0 and 100; the higher the number, the more pronounced the effect.

The Wide Aperture option in the dialog box takes into account the portions of the image outside the selected area when the filter is applied. If you choose it, the blend operation will probably take longer, but the blends may be smoother.

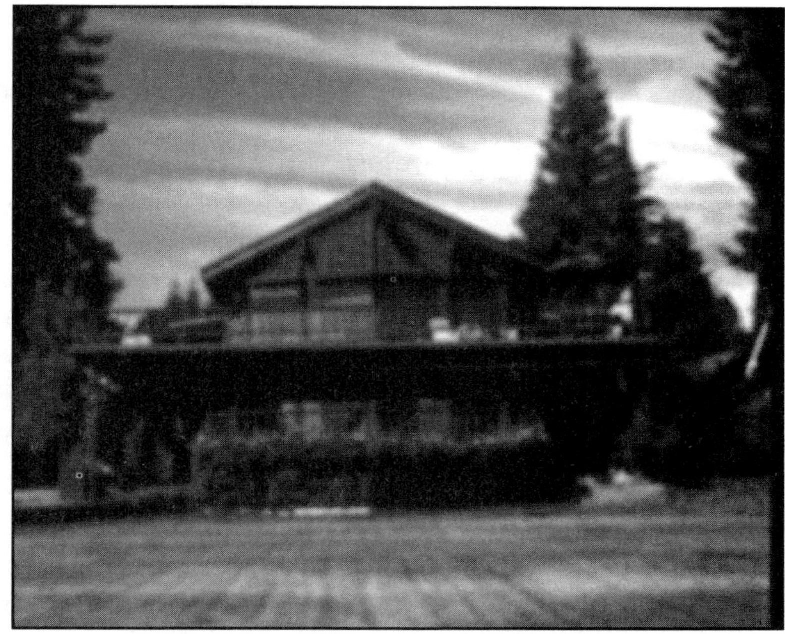

Blur

This filter (Figure 3-9) modifies the image to look as if it were shot through an out-of-focus lens. You can choose from Light, Medium, or Heavy blur effects, or create your own custom effect. To create a custom effect, enter a number from 1 (minimal blur) to 6 (maximum blur). PhotoFinish divides the image into separate "blocks"—the size of which are determined by the number you enter—and changes the center dot in each block to match the average gray or color values of the other dots in the block.

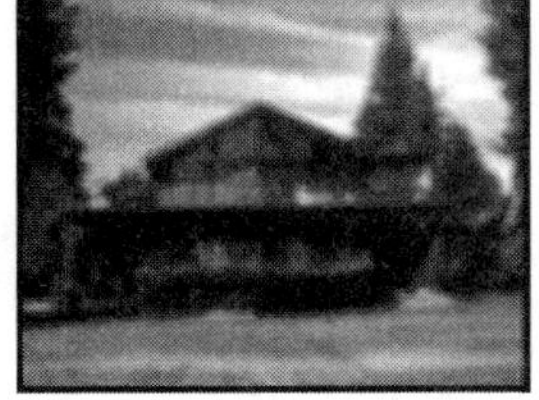

Figure 3-9. The Blur filter.

Diffuse

This filter (Figure 3-10) produces small random shifts in the pixels in an image. Imagine a sandbox in which images are formed from particles of colored sand. Applying the diffusion filter is like shaking the sandbox to scatter the particles. As you apply the filter repeatedly, the image takes on the look of a drawing.

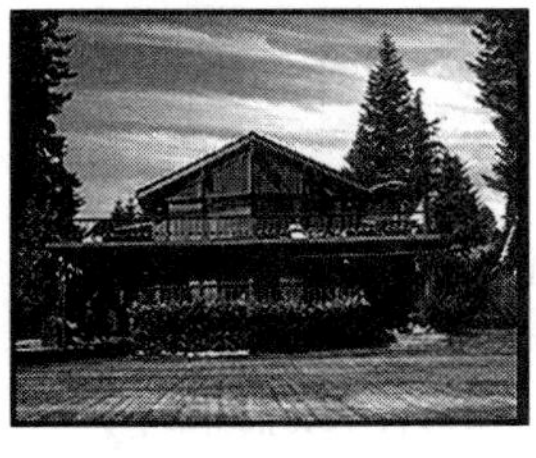

Figure 3-10. The Diffuse filter.

Again, you can select from Light, Medium, or Heavy diffusion or enter your own custom setting. The number you enter for the custom setting determines how far the dots are scattered. If you check Apply Color Shift, the filter causes new colors to be created as the pixels are redistributed.

Maximum/Minimum

These filters work like a combination brightness control/blur tool. The Maximum filter has the effect of brightening the image by emphasizing lighter areas and causing them to blur into darker areas. The Minimum filter has the opposite effect, darkening the image by emphasizing the darker areas at the expense of lighter shades. For each of these filters, you can choose from Light Medium, or Heavy options or enter your own custom values.

Posterize

This filter (Figure 3-11) reduces the number of gray shades or colors in an image, causing it to appear more like a painting than a photograph. There are four options: bilevel, 4 levels, 10 levels, or Custom.

If you choose custom, you can enter a number of levels from 2 to 64. When you apply the filter, it forces all of the pixels in the image into one of the selected number of levels.

For example, if you choose four levels in a gray-scale image, it is converted into an image consisting of four shades of gray. Each pixel in the original image is converted to one of these four shades depending on how light or dark it is.

Remove Moire

This is a very useful filter that permits you to do something only a few other programs can do: produce a gray-scale or 24-bit image from a scanned halftone.

A halftone, as we have seen, is a printed image composed of dots. These dots are printed at various angles and at various "line screens," a measure of their resolution. The dots in light areas of the image are relatively small, while the dots in darker areas are relatively large. This variation in size creates an illusion of tonality: the image appears to have multiple shades of gray or color.

Desktop scanners are designed to capture images from continuous-tone photographs, not halftones. Continuous-tone photographs consist of microscopic particles, each of which can be an almost infinite range of color. When a scanner captures a continuous-tone image, it records each dot as being a certain shade of gray (or a certain combination of RGB). But when the scanner captures a halftone, each dot is either on or off: there is no variation in intensity.

The moire-removal filter looks at this dot pattern and figures out what the halftone would have looked like as a continuous-tone image. If the dots in a certain area are relatively small, the filter converts them into relatively light shades. If the dots are large, they become dark shades. Because the filter is essentially melting these dots together, there is some loss of detail.

As with most of the other filters, you can apply this effect in one of three degrees: Light, Medium, or Heavy. You can also enter custom values between 1 (minimum effect) and 6 (maximum

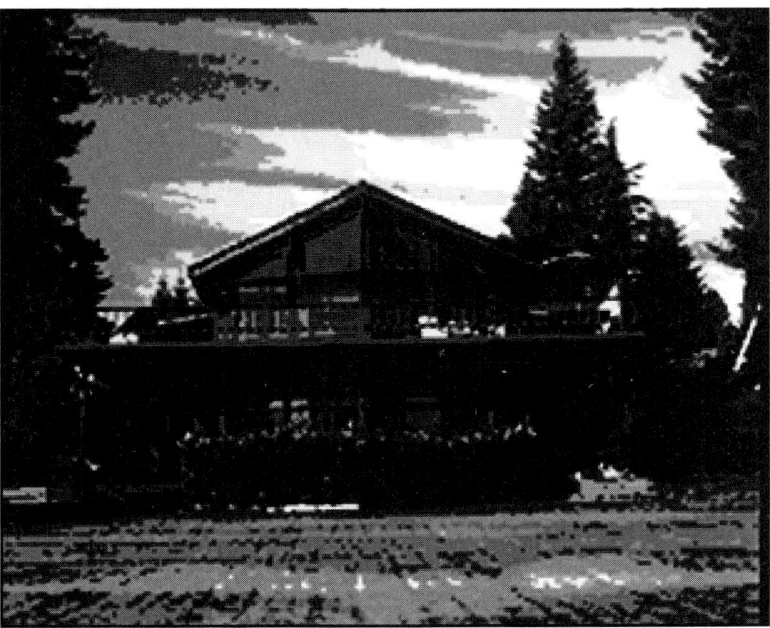

Figure 3-11. The Posterize filter reduces the number of shades in the image, making it appear more like a painting.

effect). You can apply the filter to varying degrees within the same image by selecting different portions for different levels of moire removal.

Moire removal is also available as part of the PhotoFinish AutoEnhance function. If you choose the moire removal option when you run AutoEnhance, you shouldn't have to do it again.

This is a powerful function, and like all things that are powerful, it has its dangers. Now that you can scan halftones and convert them into reasonable-looking images, you may be tempted to borrow pictures from your local newspaper or favorite magazine.

Remember that most published photographs are subject to copyright protection. Using them without the permission of the copyright holder can land you in a heap of legal trouble, especially if you publish a for-profit publication.

Remove Spots

The remove spots filter is unique in that it works with 256-color or 24-bit images, but not with gray-scale images. This filter searches the image for spots or blotches and removes them. You can choose to have it remove large, medium, or small spots.

Removing large spots takes the longest amount of time. Be forewarned that if your picture includes large splotches of paint—or your favorite dog—the Remove Spots filter could have unintended consequences.

Sharpen

The Sharpen filter is the opposite of the Blend filter. Where the Blend filter softens the boundaries between light and dark areas, Sharpen emphasizes the edges, bringing out greater detail. As with the Blend filter, you can choose from Light, Medium, or Heavy application of the effect.

You can also customize the effect by adding a value between 0 and 100; the higher the number, the more pronounced the

Sharpening. The filter also features a Wide Aperture option similar to the one available for the Blend filter.

Special Effects

The PhotoFinish filters can produce a wide range of special effects, but their primary use is to fix problems common to many images. The Special Effects, on the other hand, are pure fun. They can produce a wide range of radical transformations, converting a boring photograph into something that looks like it belongs in a museum of contemporary art.

The Special Effects are similar to the Filters in that they modify the pixels in the image to create a desired effect. Most Special Effects can be modified by making selections or entering values in the effect's dialog box. You can apply the effects to the entire image or just to a selected portion.

Version 3.0 of PhotoFinish includes two new Special Effects: "Apply Paper" and "Crumple."

Apply Paper modifies the image to look as if it were printed on a certain type of paper. You can choose from a wide variety of paper styles, such as "Coarse Canvas," "Fine Canvas," "Linen," and "Sandpaper." You can also determine the direction of the grain and the amount of smoothness or roughness. PhotoFinish 3.0 provides the same paper effects for many of the tools, which are described in Chapter Four.

Crumple acts like its name: the effects distorts the image as if it were printed on a piece of crumpled paper. As with the other effects, you have many options for how the image is "crumpled." The other effects, which are available in versions 2.0 and 3.0, are described on the following pages.

Apply Texture

This effect (Figure 3-12) superimposes a texture on top of the image. The texture itself is a gray-scale image. When you select the Apply Texture option, a dialog box allows you to load a

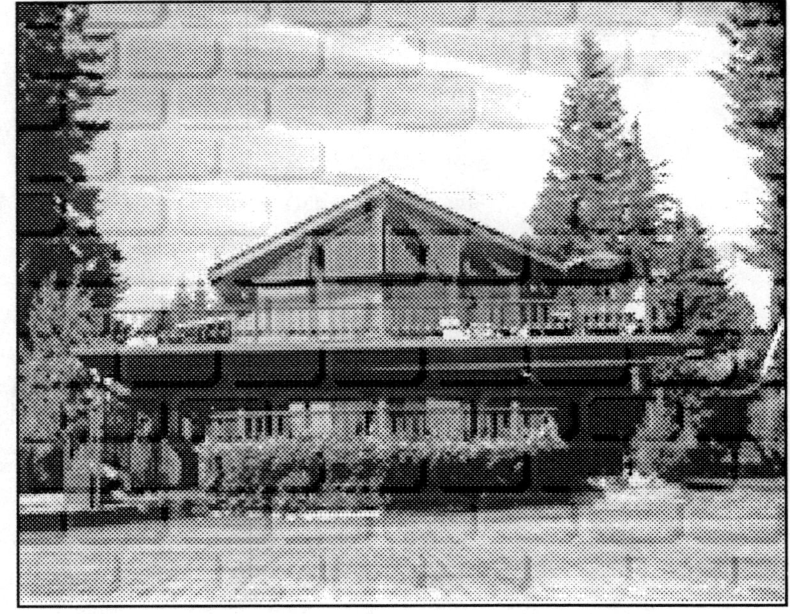

previously saved texture. You can use one of several textures installed along with PhotoFinish or create your own.

By default, the textures are stored in a Textures subdirectory to the Photo (PhotoFinish) directory. You can also choose from Light, Medium, or Heavy application of the texture, or enter a number from 1 to 100 to designate a custom level of application. The heavier the effect, the more pronounced the texture. An Invert Texture option creates a reversed version of the texture, as if it were a negative of a photograph. In PhotoFinish 3.0, this effect is known as "Texturize."

Black Hole

This effect draws the entire picture toward the center. It's as if the picture were printed on rubber and you were squeezing it at the middle. It is the opposite of the Fish-Eye Lens effect (Figure 3-13), which pulls the center of the image out to the edges. With both effects, you can choose from Light, Medium, or Heavy application, or enter a custom value.

Both effects take longer to complete than the other effects,

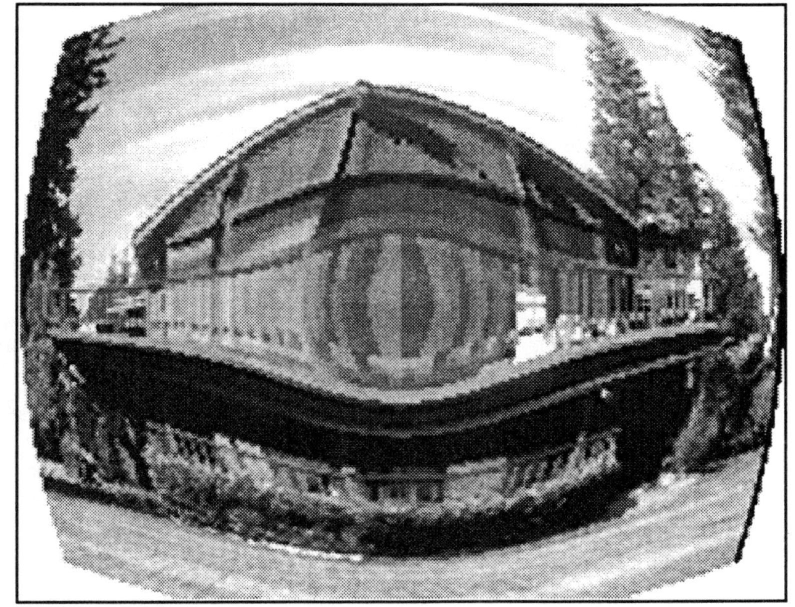

Figure 3-13. The Fish-Eye Lens effect makes it appear that the image was shot through a fish-eye lens.

though performance is improved if your computer has a math co-processor (remember, despite the pretty pictures, there is still math going on here).

Crystallize

This is one of several special effects in PhotoFinish that can convert a photographic image into what looks like a painting. This effect (Figure 3-14) identifies areas of the image with similar colors and accentuates them, making them appear to be painted.

You can choose from Light, Medium, or Heavy application, or enter a custom value, in this case from one to six.

Edge Detect

This effect identifies the edges between objects in an image and de-emphasizes everything else. The result is a version of the image that resembles a line drawing. You can choose from Sensitivity levels ranging from 1 to 10; the higher the number, the more edges get emphasized. You can also choose colors or gray levels for the outlines and background.

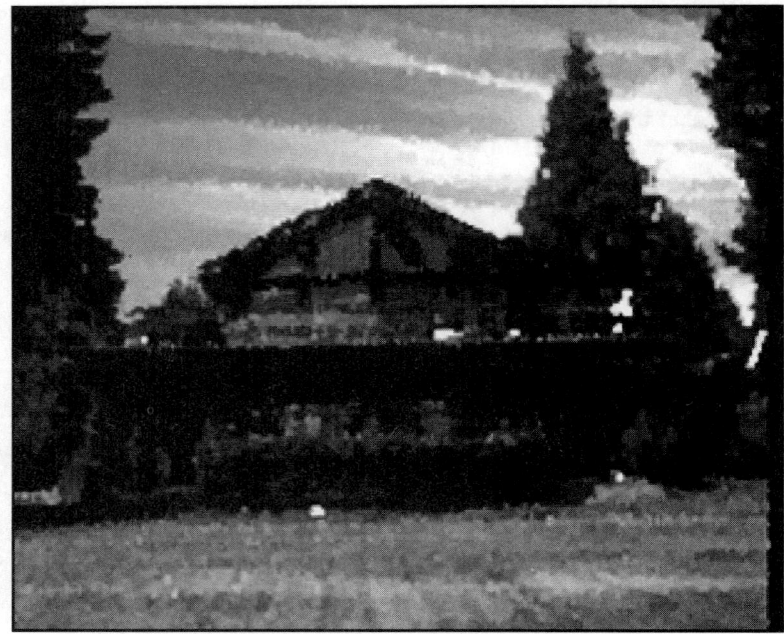

Emboss

This effect (Figure 3-15) converts the image into what appears to be a raised relief (like the impression on a rubber stamp). To enhance the 3D illusion, the effect adds shadows and highlights to the image, as if a light source were shining on it. You determine the angle of the shadows and highlights by choosing a Direction for the light source.

You also need to choose a single color for the embossed effect. Medium-gray tones, such as gray-blue, are recommended for the most pleasing visual results. Again, experiment to see what you like.

Facet

This effect causes the image to look as if it were being viewed through a multi-faceted gem. You can choose from Light, Medium, or Heavy, or enter a custom value from one to six.

Fish-Eye Lens

This effect (Figure 3-13) is the opposite of the Black Hole effect described earlier. It as if the picture were printed on rubber and

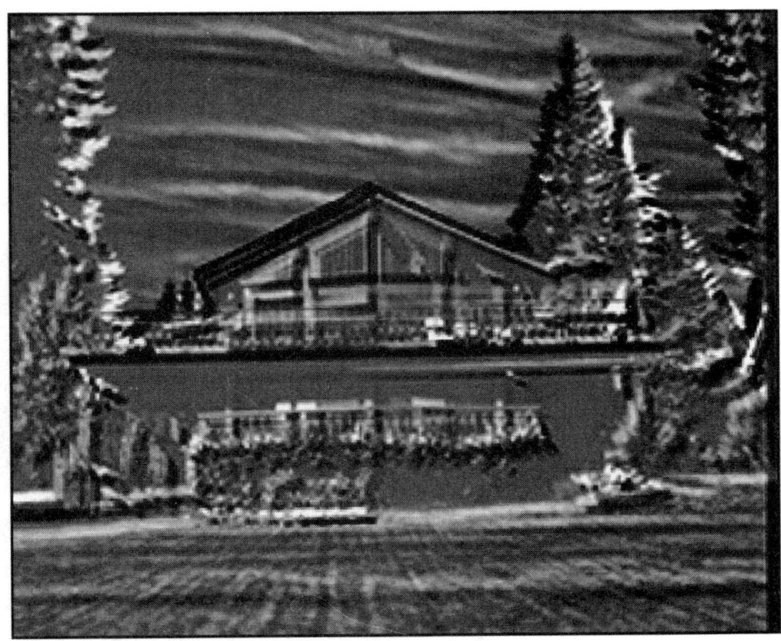

you were squeezing it at the middle. You can choose from Light, Medium, or Heavy application, or enter a custom value. Like the Black Hole, it takes longer to complete than the other effects.

Mosaic

This effect applies a mosaic pattern—a series of blocks—to the image. The image looks as if it were a completed jigsaw puzzle in which the pieces all have rectangular shapes. You can choose from small, medium, or large block sizes.

Motion Blur

This effect (Figure 3-16) makes the image look as if it were photographed at a high rate of speed. It creates an especially interesting look if you select one object in the image, such as a person, for application of the effect.

You can choose the direction of the blur and a "speed" ranging from 1 to 50, where 1 is slow and 50 is fast.

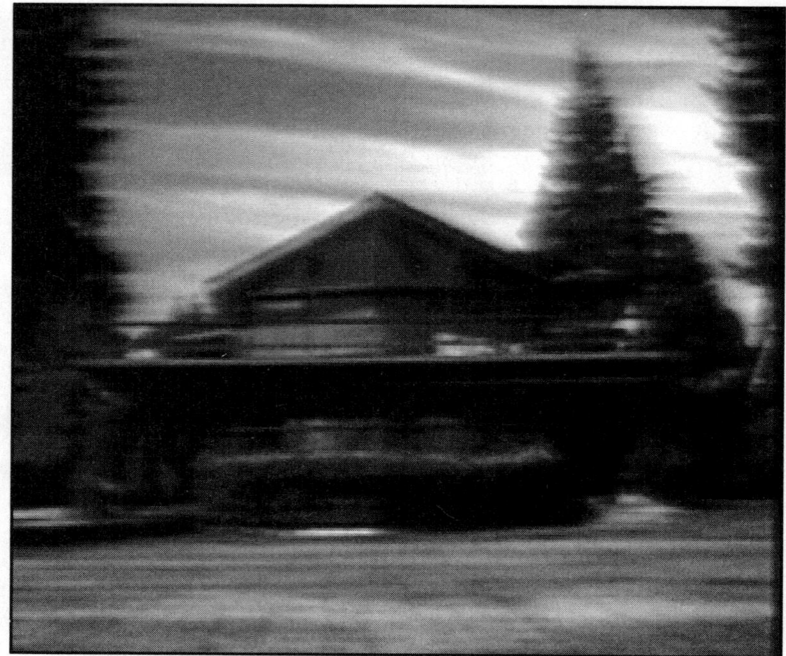

Outline

This is similar to the Edge Enhance effect, except it completely eliminates the background area instead of just de-emphasizing it. You can choose a color for the background area.

Pixelate

This effect (Figure 3-17) converts the image into a series of relatively large box-like pixels, as if its resolution were drastically reduced. It's similar to what you see if you zoom in on a bit-mapped image to the maximum level.

It's also similar to the effect you see on television news shows where they interview someone who doesn't want their face shown. You can choose from Light, Medium, or Heavy application, which essentially affect the size of the boxes. You can also enter a custom value from 1 to 16.

Twist

This effect (Figure 3-18) rotates blocks of colors in the image. You can choose the size of the blocks by entering a value from

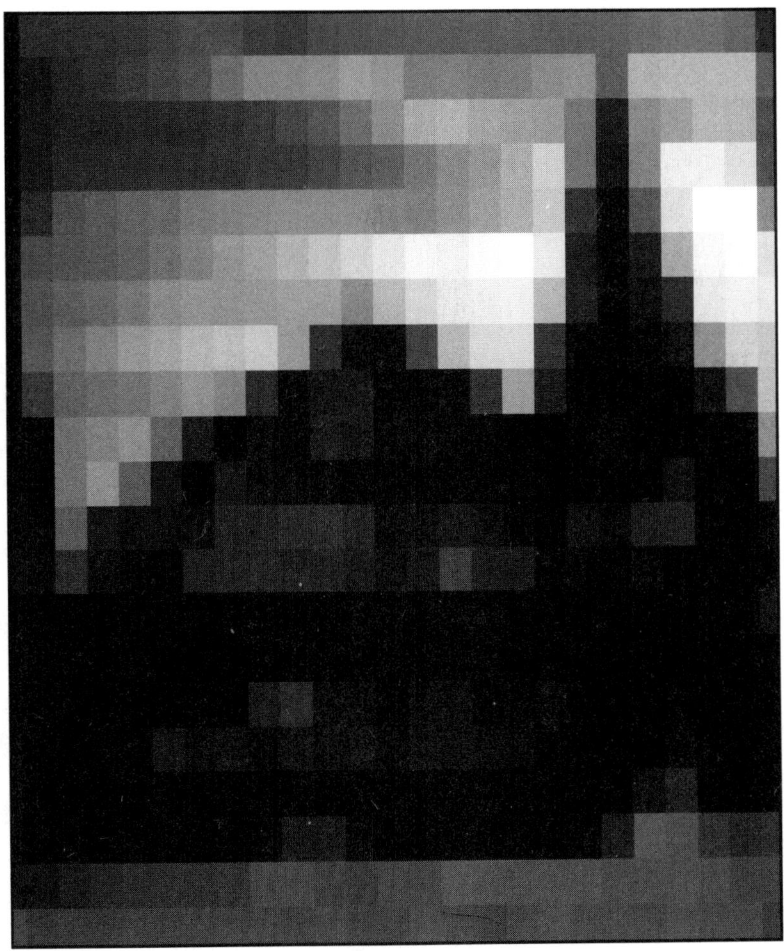

1 to 10, and you can choose the angle at which they should be rotated.

Tune

The Tune functions are much more subtle than the Filter or Special Effects functions. Rather than create radical transformations to an image, the Tune functions make relatively modest adjustment intended to improve the image's general appearance. For all the power in the Filters and Special Effects, it is probably the Tune functions that will prove to be the most useful and frequently used in the long run.

There are five Tune functions: Brightness/Contrast, Color/Gray

Map, Equalize, Hue and Saturation, and Negative. Because these functions are so important, we will deal with them in greater detail in Chapter Six.

Convert To

The Convert To option in the Image menu allows you to convert an image into one of the image modes supported by PhotoFinish: black-and-white, gray-scale, 256-color, and 24-bit color. When the conversion is completed, the new image appears in a window with the name "New." You should then use the Save As command to save it under a new name. The original file remains in its unconverted state.

If you convert an image to a format that uses less information—say a 24-bit image to 256 colors—PhotoFinish simulates the missing colors by using a dithering technique. It applies this dithering automatically unless you are converting to a black-and-white format. In that case, you can choose to have the image converted into a simple silhouette or into one of two halftone patterns: "screen" or "printer." The screen halftone, which uses randomly arranged dots, looks good on screen but poor in print. The printer halftone uses relatively large, conventional halftone dots. It looks like a coarse version of the halftone you might see in a newspaper.

Transform

The Transform commands allow you to flip, rotate, or resize the image or selected portions of the image. In most cases, you begin by selecting a part of the image using the PhotoFinish selection tools, then call up the transformation command.

Flip

This transformation creates a mirror image or inverted version of an image. Flip Horizontal flips the picture along an imaginary vertical axis; the effect is a mirror image. Flip Vertical turns the image upside-down.

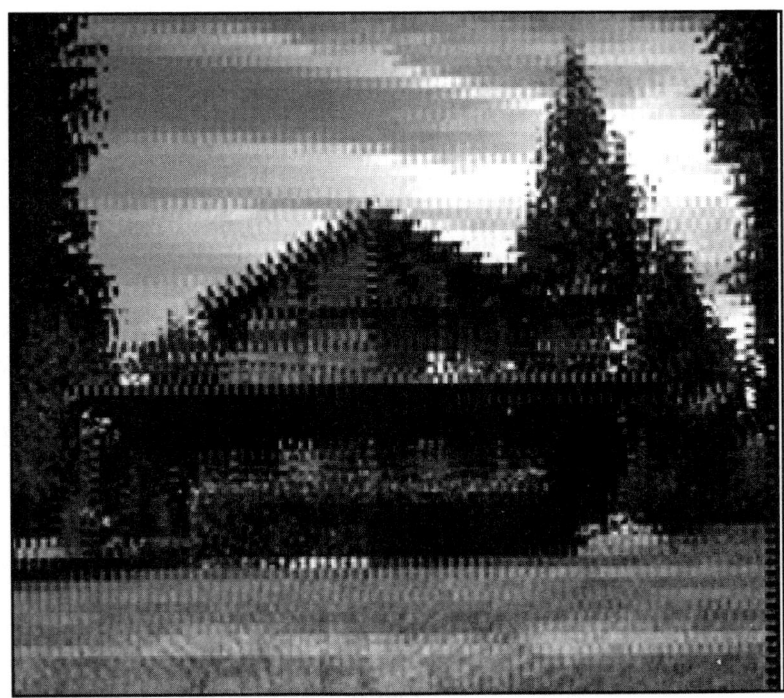

The Flip Horizontal function can be a lot of fun in combination
with the Copy and Paste commands. You can select the outline
of a person in a photograph, copy it to the Clipboard, Paste it
back in, and Flip it horizontally to create a twin.

Rotate

This command allows you to rotate the entire image or a
selected portion. You can rotate it by one of four preset
amounts—90, 180, or 270 degrees—or enter a custom value
from one to 360.

When rotating an image, many users find that they must apply
the command a few times before they get the exact degree of
rotation they want.

However, repeated application of the Rotate command creates
a blending effect. For this reason, it is a good idea to Undo the

previous rotation when experimenting with a new one. This will keep blending to a minimum.

Resize

The resize options allow you to enlarge or reduce an image or the selected portion of an image. There are two resize options: Free Resize and Resize

The Free Resize function allows you to enlarge or reduce the image visually, by dragging on handles that appear around the selected area. First, select the portion of the image you want to resize using the PhotoFinish selection tools.

Then, when you choose the Free Resize command, handles appear on the edge of the selection marquee. Place the cursor on one of the handles and hold down the mouse key to move it. Moving the handle toward the center of the image reduces it; pulling the handle away enlarges the image. If you hold down the Shift key as you drag, the program retains the ratio between the height and width of the selected image.

The Resize function allows you to reduce or enlarge an image by entering values in a dialog box. You can enter measurements for the resized image or a percentage by which the image should be enlarged or reduced.

Select the Proportion Resize option to maintain the ratio between height and width. When this option is selected, changes to the image's height or width automatically changes the value for the other dimension.

Display Menu

The Display menu provides access to commands that control how images are displayed. This is where you go if you want to zoom in or out of an image or if you want to add or remove workboxes from the screen. This is one menu where PhotoFinish 3.0 is different from version 2.0 (Figure 3-19).

Hide <u>A</u>ll Workboxes	**Ctrl+A**
✓ <u>P</u>alette	Ctrl+P
✓ <u>T</u>oolbox	Ctrl+T
✓ A<u>u</u>toBar	Ctrl+U
✓ <u>R</u>ibbon Bar	Ctrl+R
✓ <u>S</u>tatus Bar	Ctrl+B

The differences can be seen in the Screen Layout submenu, which allows you to determine which components of the screen layout are shown in the display. Normally, you would want to show all components of the display.

But if your screen "real estate" is limited, you may want to temporarily disable the display of layout components you do not need to see more of the image on which you are working. (You can also create space on the screen by moving the Palette and Toolbox toward the edges, or by using the Full Screen and Show Screen functions. Full Screen removes the PhotoFinish title bar and menu bar and maximizes the window to fill the screen. Show Screen removes everything except the picture, but you cannot edit the image.)

PhotoFinish 2.0 includes a Brush Width and Shape workbox that allows you to determine the width and shape of tools found in the PhotoFinish Toolbox. You use the Screen Layout option to turn the display of this box off or on. In PhotoFinish 3.0, this workbox has been eliminated. Instead, brush width and shape are set from the AutoBar or from the Tools Options dialog box.

In PhotoFinish 3.0, the Screen Layout submenu also allows you to display (or hide) the Ribbon and AutoBar. By default, the Ribbon is turned on and the AutoBar is turned off. The Ribbon provides fast access to functions you would otherwise have to select from one of the menus.

The AutoBar provides quick access to a variety of options depending on which tool is selected. For example, when you select the Text tool, the AutoBar allows you to select the style of type to be entered. Two other Screen Layout options are Crosshair and Status Bar. The Crosshair option enables or disables the appearance of a crosshair when you select a tool. The Status Bar option allows you to hide or show the status bar that appears on the bottom of the screen.

One of the most often used functions in the Display menu is Zoom. This command allows you to view the image at various levels of magnification. You can zoom in to do precise detail work, or zoom out to get the overall view of a large-sized image. Zoom options are also available by selecting the Zoom tool from the Toolbox. Zoom options range from 3 percent (a vastly reduced view) to 1600 percent (a vast magnification). The 100 percent zoom option at the top of the Display menu quickly returns you to the full-sized view.

The Zoom to Fit option automatically adjusts the zoom to fill the entire desktop. The Calibrate Monitor function allows you to modify the display of images to account for the particular characteristics of your monitor. It does this by presenting a series of boxes that you choose from depending on their color contrast. From this, the program builds a "transfer" curve that automatically modifies the image. This function is discussed more thoroughly in Chapter Five.

Window Menu

The Window menu in PhotoFinish is similar to the Window menus found in other Windows applications. If you have multiple windows open, you can choose which is to be the active one. You can choose how the windows are arranged on the screen through the Cascade and Tile commands. But perhaps the most useful command is Window Duplicate.

PhotoFinish allows you to open multiple versions of the same file. However, each version is considered a separate image, and modifications made to one will not be reflected in the others. The Window Duplicate command creates a window containing a duplicate of the image in the active window. Any changes made to the image in the active window will also show up in the duplicate window. This feature is especially useful if you want to zoom in on your image for detail work. By keeping the duplicate image at its normal size, you can see the effects of any changes you make while the original image is magnified.

Remember our earlier warning about the Active Picture Window. This is the currently selected window, the one affected by the current image operation. You can have multiple windows for each file, each of which can have different effects applied to them. If you want to save a particular version of an image, you must select that window to make it active, then use Save As to save it.

Having covered the PhotoFinish menus, we can look at the other home for its features: its workboxes.

CHAPTER 4

· ·

PhotoFinish Workboxes

We have seen that the PhotoFinish menus provide access to a wide range of features for modifying and enhancing images. But some of the most powerful tools the program has to offer are found in its workboxes.

PhotoFinish 2.0 uses three workboxes: the Toolbox, Width and Shape, and Palette (Figure 4-1). Version 3.0 eliminates the Width and Shape workbox in favor of an AutoBar. The toolbox includes display, selection, painting, and retouch tools. The Width and Shape box (AutoBar in version 3.0) allows the user to adjust the size and shape of the Paintbrush and other tools. The Palette allows the user to select the colors to be applied by the painting tools.

The Toolbox is the most important of the workboxes. But before we discuss the tools, we should first look at how colors are selected in PhotoFinish. We will therefore begin with a discussion of the PhotoFinish Palette.

Palette

We have all seen the traditional artist's palette on which a painter mixes the various colors that will be used for a piece of artwork. The PhotoFinish Palette is the electronic equivalent of the traditional palette. It is a rectangular grid that displays up to 256 colors available for application to the image.

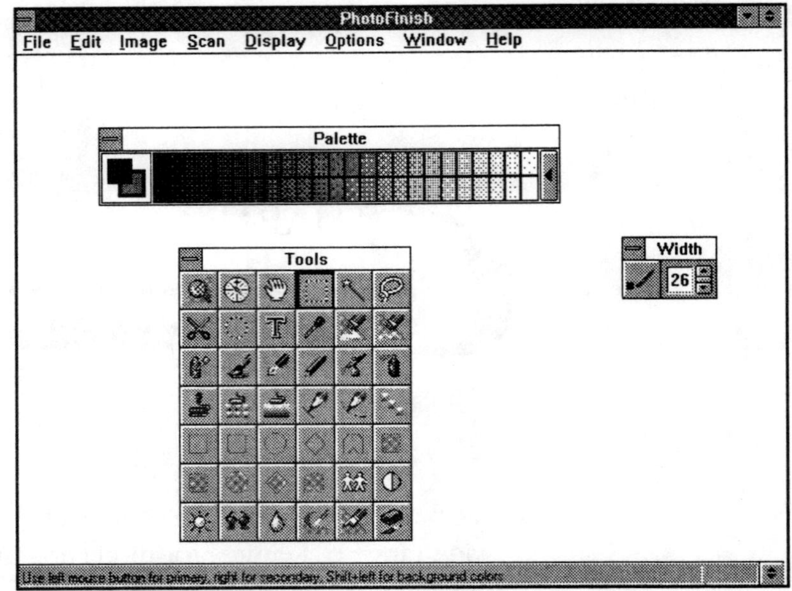

If you are working in 8-bit gray-scale or color mode, the palette will include all of the colors or gray shades available to you. If you are working in 24-bit color mode, the palette is a random selection of the 16.7 million colors available to you. You can change any of the colors in the 24-bit palette by double-clicking on a color. Exactly how this is done is explained below.

The PhotoFinish Palette acts like any other standard window. By default, it appears at the bottom of the screen, but you can move it to another part of the screen by dragging it with the mouse. You can close the palette by double-clicking on the little horizontal slot that appears in the upper left-hand corner. To make the palette reappear, go to the Display menu and select Palette from the Screen Layout sub-menu. You can also "fold," or reduce the physical size of the palette, by clicking on the arrow that appears to its right. Click on the arrow again to "unfold" the palette.

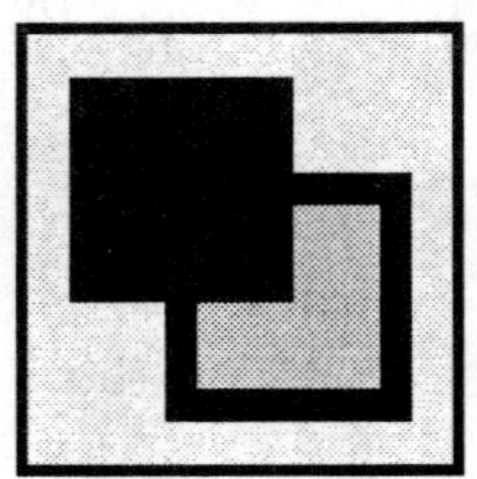

Figure 4-2. The Color Selection Box in the Palette allows you to select the Primary color (box, upper left), Seondary Color (box, lower right), and Background Color (background).

To the left of the palette is a Color Selection Box (Figure 4-2) that shows the three currently selected colors: primary, secondary, and background. These are the colors that will be applied depending on which tool you are using.

The primary color is applied when you use one of the basic painting tools, such as the Paintbrush or Fountain Pen. The primary color also forms the boundary of shapes created with the shape tools, which are explained below. It is displayed in the top square within the Color Selection Box.

The secondary color, which appears in the bottom square, is the color that fills shapes created with the Text or filled shape tools. The background color, which appears in the background of the Color Selection Box, is used with the Eraser and Gradient Paint tools.

You can select primary, secondary, and background colors either by clicking on a color in the palette or by using the Eyedropper tool in the toolbox. The Eyedropper tool allows you to select a color from your artwork simply by pointing at it and clicking.

Whether you use the Eyedropper or the Palette, you use the same procedure for selecting the primary, secondary, and background colors. To select the primary color, click on the left mouse button as you are pointing to the color you want to select. To select the secondary color, click on the right mouse button. To select the background color, hold down the Shift key and click on the left mouse button. Verify that you have selected the correct color by looking at the Color Selection Box.

When using the Eyedropper tool to select colors, you have the option of selecting the color of the single pixel you are pointing at, or the average color of the surrounding pixels.

The easiest way to choose among these options is to double-click on the Eyedropper tool. A dialog box appears allowing you to choose Single Pixel or the range of pixels that should be used to select the average color. You can also call up the same dialog box by clicking once on the Eyedropper tool, then selecting Tool Options from the Options menu.

We noted above that when working in 24-bit color mode, you

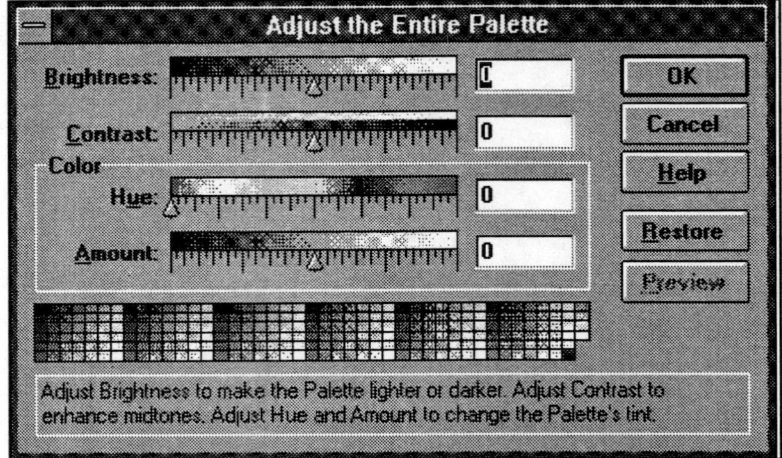

can change the colors in the palette by double-clicking on any color within the grid. When you do this, the PhotoFinish Color Picker appears. This allows you to create your own color using the HLS, RGB, or CYM color models described in Chapter One. Once you have selected the color you want, it replaces the color that you clicked on.

The PhotoFinish Options menu includes several selections that allow you to modify your Palette in other ways.

The Palette All Colors option (Figure 4-3) allows you to make global changes to your palette. You can adjust the overall brightness and contrast by dragging on the appropriate arrows in the dialog box or by entering values from -100 to +100. You can also adjust the hue by entering a number from 0 to 360, just as you would if you were using the HLS color model in the

Color Picker dialog box. In 256-color mode, the Palette All Colors dialog box changes the range of colors available for that file. As a result, the colors in the image will change. You can see just how they will change by using the Preview option. In 24-bit color mode, the dialog box merely changes the colors that will be displayed in the Palette. It has no effect on the image.

The Color Picker option brings up the same Color Picker dialog box that appeared when you double-clicked on a color in the Palette. You can adjust the primary color or select another color to adjust. The Range of Colors dialog box allows you to select a range of colors to include in the Palette, which is useful when creating gradient effects. You select a beginning color and an end color and the program adds colors in between.

The Single Colors dialog box (Figure 4-4) allows you to change individual colors. Choosing this option is much the same as double-clicking on a color in the Palette.

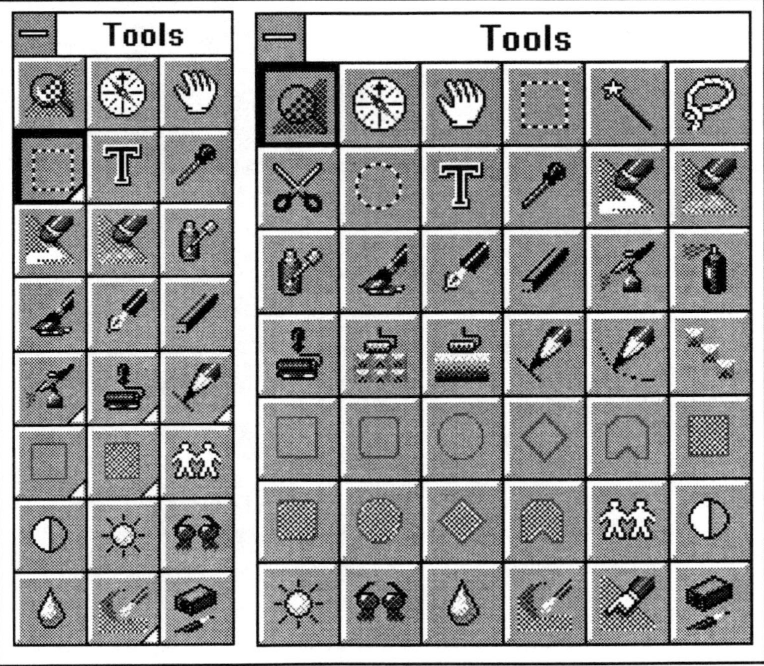

Figure 4-5. The Toolbox can be Grouped (left) or Ungrouped (right) by clicking once on the small bar in the upper left. The PhotoFinish 2.0 toolboxes are shown here.

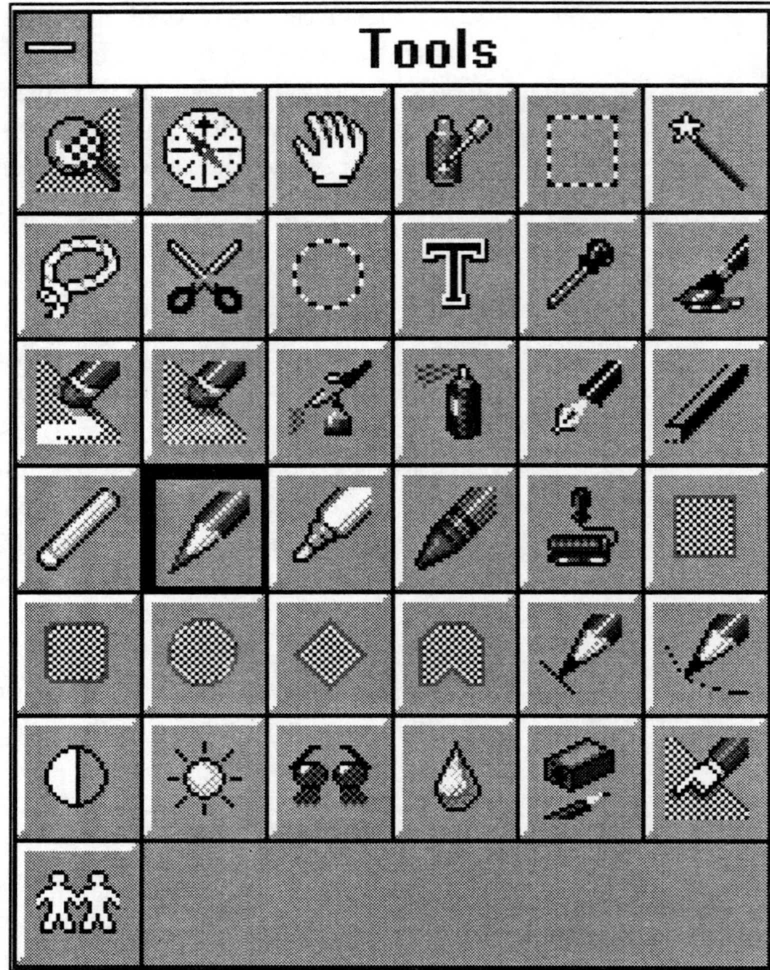

Figure 4-6. The toolbox in PhotoFinish 3.0 features fewer icons, but more options for each tool.

If you have created a custom palette, you may want to save it for use with other images. To do this, select Save As Palette from the Options menu. To load a saved palette, select Open Palette.

The Toolbox

The Toolbox is one area of PhotoFinish that received a major upgrade in the transition from version 2.0 (Figure 4-5) to version 3.0 (Figure 4-6). In addition to adding new tools, version 3.0 changes the way that tools are customized. The result is a host of new "natural media" painting capabilities.

"Natural media" tools mimick the actions of traditional artistic media like chalk, crayons, charcoal, or oil paint. PhotoFinish 2.0 includes many tools that duplicate the effects of some natural media, but version 3.0 takes this concept much further. In addition to new painting tools, PhotoFinish 3.0 allows you to simulate the effects of painting on various kinds of surfaces. When you paint on smooth paper, the effect is much different than if you were painting on a rough canvas or another textured surface. With PhotoFinish 3.0, you can select from 21 different kinds of simulated surfaces on which to paint. You can also adjust the smoothness and grain of each surface.

The Toolbox in PhotoFinish 2.0 features a total of 42 tools. PhotoFinish 3.0 reduces this to 37, but don't be fooled: there are actually many more options for how you can paint or modify an image. Some tools that were separate functions in version 2.0, with their own icons in the toolbox, are now available as options for other tools in version 3.0. For example, version 2.0 included three kinds of paint roller tools that have now been combined into one.

The Toolbox itself is a collection of icons that normally displays 24 PhotoFinish tools. However, tools with similar functions are grouped together under a single icon to save space. Icons for these multi-purpose tools are identified by a small white triangle in the lower right-hand corner. Think of it as a cut-out providing access to other tools below.

When you click in the triangle, you can see icons for other tools in the group. For example, when you click in the lower right-hand corner of the box selection tool (a rectangular dotted line), you will see additional icons for other selection tools. If you drag the cursor to one of those icons, the newly selected tool appears in the Toolbox.

You can also choose to display all 42 tools in the Toolbox by Ungrouping them, or change the number of rows or columns for either a Grouped or Ungrouped Toolbox. Do this by clicking once on the small bar in the upper left corner of the

Toolbox (be careful—if you double-click, you will close the box, and will have to reopen it using the Screen Layout option in the Display menu).

When you click on the bar, you will see a short menu of options. Choose Layout from the bottom of the menu. Select Ungroup if you want to display all the tools, or Group to go back to the reduced Toolbox.

You can also choose the number of rows or columns in which the Toolbox will be displayed if you would like to change this. The number of rows you select will determine the number of columns and vice-versa. For example, if you choose four columns in a Grouped Toolbox, it will have six rows. Choose six columns for an Ungrouped Toolbox and it will have seven rows.

In addition to new options, PhotoFinish 3.0 offers a new approach to modifying the effects of tools through the AutoBar. When you select a tool, most of the options for using it are displayed in the AutoBar (provided you have selected "AutoBar" from the Screen Layout submenu of the Display menu). This makes it easier and faster to access these options. The Toolbox is divided into four categories: display, selection, painting, and retouch tools.

Display Tools

The toolbox includes three tools designed to enhance the use of the display: the zoom tool, locator tool, and hand tool.

Zoom

The Zoom tool provides the same magnification and reduction options found in the Zoom menu command. The advantage of the zoom tool is that you can zoom in on a particular portion of an image without using the window scroll bars. Select the tool and move it to the area you want to zoom in on (or out from). Click on the left mouse button to zoom in and the right mouse button to zoom out. If you continue to hit the right or left mouse buttons, the image zooms in or out to its next available increment of enlargement or reduction. Reduction (zoom out) options are 3, 6, 12, 25, 33, and 50 percent. Enlargement (zoom in) options are 200, 300, 400, 600, 800, 1000, and 1600 percent. When you select the Zoom tool, various zoom options appear in the AutoBar. These options correspond to the zoom options in the Display menu.

Locator

This tool is used if you have opened one or more duplicate windows. One window might include a zoomed-out view of the entire image, while another presents a magnified view of a small portion of the same picture.

The idea is that you can do detail work in the magnified view while keeping a perspective on the overall appearance of your work. Using the Locator tool, you click in the window containing the reduced view of the entire image. The magnified view then moves to the portion of the image on which you clicked in the reduced view.

Hand

The hand tool allows you to move the image within the Active Window. You can accomplish the same feat with the scroll bars, but the hand tool offers greater freedom in the direction in which you can move the picture.

Selection Tools

PhotoFinish's selection tools are an important component of the program. They allow you to select a portion of the image for further image processing applications. Once a portion of the image is selected, you can copy it to the Clipboard, drag it around the screen, or modify it with one of PhotoFinish's filters or special effects. A portion of an image selected for one of these operations is known as a "cut-out."

You can tell that it is selected because it is surrounded by an animated dotted line known as a "marquee."

There are five selection tools in all. They are grouped together in the Toolbox, with the box selection tool the default. To access the other selection tools, move the cursor to the small white triangle in the corner of the icon and hold down the mouse button.

The box, lasso, scissors, and elliptical selection tools are all very similar. Each allows you to draw a marquee around the portion of the image to be selected.

The box tool draws a rectangular marquee. You select the tool, place the cursor at one corner of where you want the cut-out to begin, hold down the mouse key, then drag to the opposite corner. The elliptical tool draws an oval or circle.

The lasso tool is used to draw a freehand marquee: just drag it around the object you want to select.

The scissors tool is used to create marquees in the shape of polygons, that is, shapes consisting of straight lines. Click at the point where you want the marquee to begin, then at a second point, a third, and so on. Each time you click, a line is added between the last point and the current one. When you surround the object and click again at the first point, the marquee is completed.

The Magic Wand works a little differently. This tool allows you

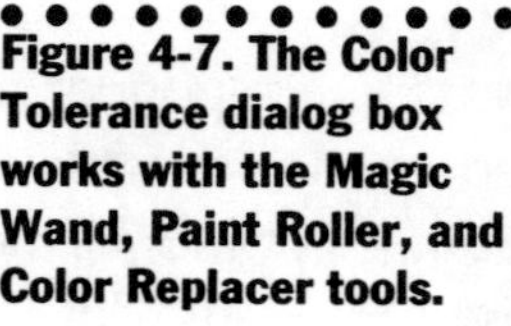

Figure 4-7. The Color Tolerance dialog box works with the Magic Wand, Paint Roller, and Color Replacer tools.

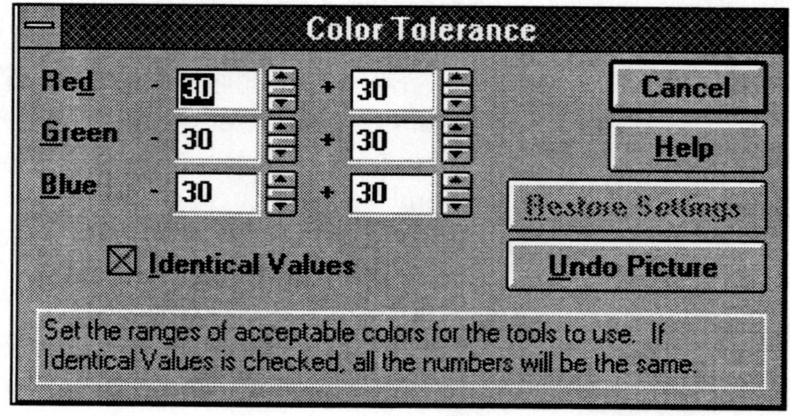

to automatically select an irregular object by simply clicking inside it. It works best when the colors or gray shades within the object have similar values and there is a high degree of contrast with the surrounding area.

The Magic Wand is one of three tools that can be modified using the Color Tolerance dialog box, which is accessed by double-clicking on the tool or selecting the Color Tolerance option from the Options menu (Figure 4-7). When used in combination with the Color Tolerance dialog box, the Magic Wand allows you to define the range of colors that will be selected. Because this dialog box has multiple applications—and because the concept is a little tricky—we'll spend a little time discussing it.

Remember from Chapter One that a computer treats colors as just another form of numbers. Any color that can be displayed on your monitor can be described as a combination of red, green, and blue. Thus, in a 24-bit image, a color can be expressed as a combination of three values, each ranging from zero (the least intense shade of that color) to 256 (the most intense). A shade of purple, for example, might be 167 red, 47 green, and 170. You can experiment with these numbers yourself using the Single Color option in the Palette submenu of the Options dialog box.

The Color Tolerance dialog box allows you to define the range of colors that will be affected by the Magic Wand, Color Replacer, and Paint Roller tools. It allows you to enter two sets of numbers: one for the lower range of colors to be affected, the other for the upper range. When you enter the RGB numbers, the Magic Wand will select only the shades that fall between those RGB values.

ZSoft recommends that you enter "30" for all of the numbers and leave it at that. But if you want to experiment with different settings, try this:

Using the Eyedropper tool (described below), you can see the color values for any color in the image. Just select the tool and pass it over the color you want to measure. The RGB values appear in the status bar at the bottom of the screen. When using the Magic Wand tool, find the color values for the region of the image bordering on the area you want to select. Then find the values for the area within that border—the area you want to select. By entering those two sets of RGB values in the Color Tolerance dialog box, you can determine the scope of the Magic Wand selection. This works best if there is a high degree of contrast between the two areas, and will probably require some experimentation. But this method provides a valuable way to automate the selection process.

Once a cut-out is selected, you can perform many operations on it using menu selections, including the Filters and Special Effects. You can also copy cut-outs to the Clipboard or to a file.

PhotoFinish offers several options for pasting and dragging cut-outs. The Select Transparent option in the Edit menu makes the background of a cut-out transparent when you paste it in. If you drag a cut-out from one portion of an image to another, you can make the background transparent by holding down the right mouse button as you drag. The Select Leave Original Option leaves a copy of the cut-out in its original position when you drag it elsewhere.

The Crop command in the Edit menu automatically crops away the portion of the image outside the cut-out. The cropped image is displayed in a new window that appears on top of the original. This is a good way to reduce the size of a file if you find that you do not need the entire image. Be sure to close the original or you will lose the memory benefits of the smaller image.

Modifying the Painting Tools

PhotoFinish 2.0 and 3.0 both provide a wide range of painting tools that simulate the actions of such traditional artist's tools as paintbrushes, airbrushes, and charcoal. They also include tools for drawing standard geometric shapes and for filling shapes with selected colors or patterns.

The painting tools in PhotoFinish are quite versatile. They include all of the tools you would expect to find in a painting program like PC Paintbrush, allowing you to create original artwork from scratch. But they can also be used to touch up or add special effects to an existing image.

However, they should not be confused with the PhotoFinish Retouch Tools, which are primarily intended for retouching photographs (more on those below).

As noted above, PhotoFinish 2.0 and 3.0 take different approaches to modifying the actions of these tools. You will find that 3.0 gives you many more options while making it easier to get the exact effect you want.

In PhotoFinish 2.0, you modify the width and shape of the painting tools using the Width and Shape workbox. By clicking on the paintbrush on the left of the box, you can select from several brush shapes. The number on the right indicates the width of the brush. You can enter a number, click on the up or down arrows to increase or decrease the size, or position the cursor in between the arrows and drag it up or down to change the size quickly.

PhotoFinish 3.0 eliminates the Width and Shape workbox in favor of an AutoBar that appears at the top of the screen. In addition, you can change these settings—and do much more— by double-clicking on the painting tool you want to use.

This brings up a Tool Options dialog box that offers many options for customizing the effect of the tool. One nice thing about the dialog box is that you can keep it open as you are painting in the Active Window. This allows you to experiment with different settings and combinations of settings. You can also Undo the effects created by the selected tool from within the dialog box. PhotoFinish 2.0 offers a Tool Options dialog box for many tools, but not all of them (Figure 4-8). Tools that can be modified are known as "soft tools," and include the Paintbrush, Airbrush, Smear Paintbrush, Charcoal, and Clone function.

Modifying Tools in Version 2.0

We will begin by describing the Soft Tool options in PhotoFinish 2.0. Even if you use 3.0, it is a good idea to read this section, because we will refer to it in our discussion of the later version.

Edge. This setting allows you to determine the degree to which the painting tool "bleeds" from its edges. You have three options: hard, medium, and soft. "Hard" creates a hard edge, "soft" creates a soft edge, and "medium" creates an edge in between the two. The soft edge creates something of a water color effect with certain tools. PhotoFinish 3.0 does not include an edge setting, but some of the new tool options available in the upgrade give the same effect as setting the edge to soft, medium, or hard.

Density. This setting determines the intensity of the tool's effect. You can choose a value between -100 and +100. The lower the number, the less the intensity.

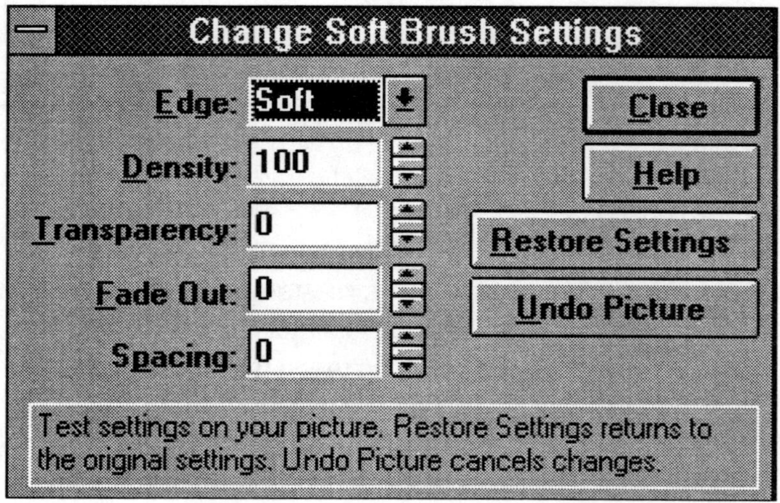

Figure 4-8. The Change Soft Brush Settings dialog box in PhotoFinish 2.0 allows you to adjust settings for the Paintbrush, Charcoal, Airbrush, and Clone tools. This dialog box provides options for the Paintbrush tool.

Setting a low density has a similar effect to setting a small brush width. If you hold the tool over a portion of an image without moving it and continually click on the mouse button (or just hold it down in the case of the Airbrush), the paint gradually grows to fill the entire width of the brush. At a low density, the paint effect slowly builds until it fills the entire width of the brush. At a high density, the paint fills the width of the brush more quickly.

Transparency. The Transparency option allows you to change the relative transparency or opacity of the paint stroke. When you select a relatively high level of transparency, you can see objects over which you are painting. A value of 0 makes the paint totally opaque, while a value of 100 makes it totally transparent. If you set your tool to make it totally transparent, you'll be wasting your time, because it won't have any effect.

Fade-out. Fade-out makes the tool act as if you were painting on a canvas and slowly lifted the brush as you were making the stroke (Figure 4-9). The effect is that the paint stroke fades toward the end. You can choose a number from 0 to 100. The higher the number, the greater the fade-out. This is another setting not found in PhotoFinish 3.0 because many of the tool options have the same effect.

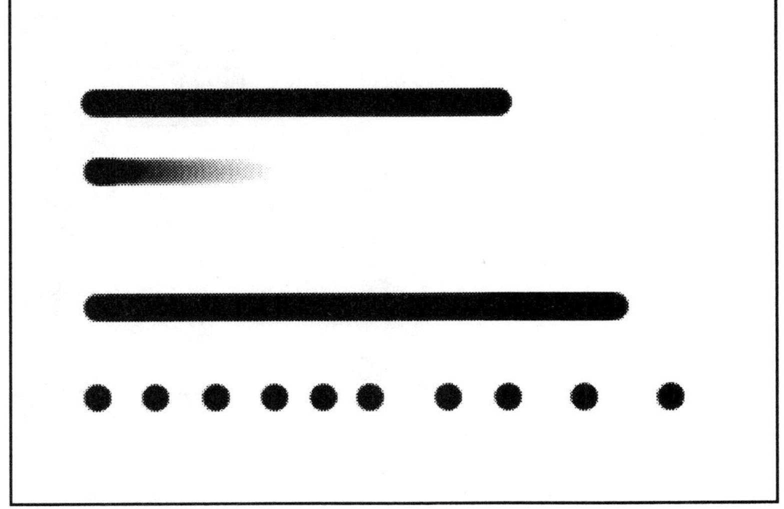

Figure 4-9. The Fade-Out in PhotoFinish 2.0 option determines the degree to which the paint dissipates. The Spacing option determines the space between dots as you paint.

Spacing. Here, you can create effects similar to what would happen if you sporadically lifted the brush off the canvas as you were painting. Again, you can enter a value from 0 to 100. The higher the number, the greater the space between dabs of electronic paint. For the smoothest effect, you should select a value that is one-fourth your brush size.

You can also use the Soft Tool Settings dialog box to modify the rate of flow of the Airbrush tool or to adjust the way the Clone tool works. These options will be discussed when we cover those respective tools.

Modifying Tools in Version 3.0

PhotoFinish 3.0 offers much more flexibility in determining tool settings while making it easier to choose from various options. These options are selected from a dialog box that appears when you double-click on the tool or select "Tool Options" from the Options dialog box (Figure 4-10).

The dialog box varies for each tool, but most have certain settings in common. For example, most tools offer four transparency options: "Sheer," "Dense," "Solid," and "Custom." "Sheer" is equivalent to a transparency setting of 85, while "dense" is equivalent to 30 and "solid" is zero (not transparent

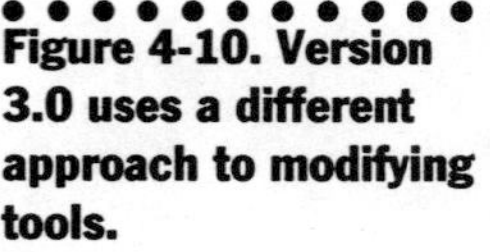

Figure 4-10. Version 3.0 uses a different approach to modifying tools.

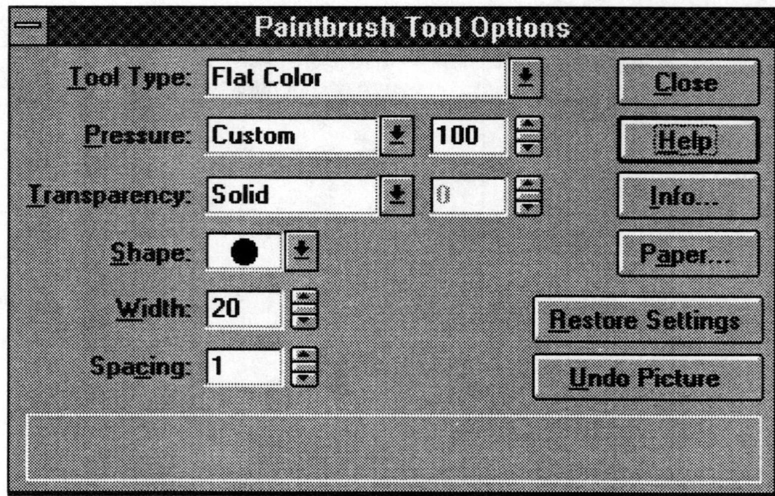

at all). You can also enter a custom setting from 0 to 100, just as you can in PhotoFinish 2.0.

Most tools also offer "Pressure" settings corresponding to how hard you would hold a traditional artist's tool against the surface. Again, each of these settings has a numeric equivalent, and you can also enter a custom number from zero to 100. The settings are "Light" (25), "Medium" (50), and "Heavy" (75).

Most of the tools in 3.0 also have a "Spacing" option that works pretty much the way it does in version 2.0.

In addition to these settings, most of the painting tools in PhotoFinish 3.0 have variations on the basic effect of the tool. Some of these variations are simply a specific combination of transparency, pressure, and spacing settings, while others modify the effect of the tool in other ways. As always, it is a good idea to experiment with these variations to see their effects.

One final—and very powerful—setting is the option to choose from 21 types of "Paper" (or, more accurately, "surfaces"). You do this by clicking on the "Paper" button that appears in the Options dialog box. When you select a paper type, the painting tool will act as if you were painting on that kind of surface. For each paper type, you can also choose the smoothness and direction of the "grain." The paper types are listed below (Figure 4-11). We will not attempt to describe how each one

Bond	Halftone	Sandpaper
Coarse Canvas	Handmade	Sidewalk
Cold Press	Leather	Snakeskin
Construction	Leopard	Squiggles
Cotton	Linen	Standard
Diagonals	Lines	Vellum
Fine Canvas	Parchment	Woodgrain

works—you can see this for yourself when you choose the paper you want to use.

The Painting Tools

In this section, we will describe the specific tools in PhotoFinish, beginning with the tools in both versions, and finishing with the tools new to version 3.0. We will also note any differences in the way the tools work between the two versions.

Paintbrush

This is your basic tool for drawing solid colors on the electronic canvas. Drag it around the screen and you will see that it paints the currently selected primary color at the currently selected width in the currently selected shape. By holding down the Shift key as you paint, you can constrain the stroke to a straight vertical or horizontal line. Hit the space bar to change from vertical to horizontal or vice-versa.In version 2.0, this is a soft tool, meaning it can be modified by double-clicking on the icon or by selecting Tool Options from the Options dialog box once you have selected the tool.

PhotoFinish 3.0 offers several variations on the Basic Paintbrush, and even variations within variations:

Flat Color. This paints in a solid color, with no transparency and a pressure setting of 100.

Jitter. This is an interesting effect that works just like its name. As you paint, the brush "jumps around" to add random strokes outside its path. It's as if the brush were dancing while it's painting. "Jitter Rainbow" and "Jitter Two-Tone" combine the jitter effect with the rainbow and two-tone effects described below.

Neon. This tool creates a glowing effect when you paint over another color.

Rainbow. This tool changes in color as you paint, producing a series of colors spanning the spectrum.

Soft. This setting provides the same effect as choosing a soft edge in PhotoFinish 2.0.

Two Tone. This is similar to the Rainbow effect, but instead of creating a rainbow of colors, it creates a transition from the primary color to the secondary color.

Wash. This is a highly transparent variation of the basic brush.

Wet Oil Paint. This brush fades as you paint, as if you selected a high degree of fade-out in PhotoFinish 2.0.

Fountain Pen

This tool is primarily intended for editing individual pixels in a highly magnified view of the image. In PhotoFinish 2.0, it is not a soft tool, so its effects cannot be modified. As with the Paintbrush, you can constrain movement horizontally or vertically by holding down the Shift key. PhotoFinish 3.0 offers five variations on the Basic Pen: Ball Point, which creates a smooth drawing effect with a soft edge; Calligraphic, which uses an angled "nib" to create variations in the width of the stroke depending on the direction in which you are moving the pen; Fine, a thin pen with a soft edge; Medium, a thicker pen, also with a soft edge; and Quill, which fades as you draw. The degree to which the Quill pen fades is determined by the texture of the paper.

Charcoal

The Charcoal tool works only in gray-scale or 24-bit color mode. It paints only in black, white, or shades of gray. You can constrain movement horizontally or vertically by holding down the Shift key.

In PhotoFinish 2.0, selecting the Charcoal tool brings up a palette that allows you to select the gray shade you want to paint with. Its effects can also be modified using the Soft Tool Settings dialog box.

PhotoFinish 3.0 handles the Charcoal tool much differently.

Instead of selecting from a range of gray shades, you can modify the transparency of the tool. You can also choose from two variations: "Gritty," which is grainy, and "Soft," which is smoother (Figure 4-12).

Airbrush

The Airbrush effect is similar to a traditional airbrush: it sprays a fine "mist" of dots into the image, gradually increasing in intensity as you hold down the mouse button. The "Rate of Flow" option determines the speed at which the intensity increases as you hold the mouse button. In PhotoFinish 2.0, the tool includes a density setting: if you set a low density, the tool's effect is most intense in the center of the brush and gradually grows to fill its entire width.

PhotoFinish 3.0 adds four variations on the Basic Airbrush (Figure 4-13): The Bull's Eye creates a "target" effect when the tool is applied in a stationary manner, with alternating light and dark rings; the Fat Tip creates a heavy edge with a high rate of flow; the Feather Tip has a lighter edge; and the Ring applies a heavy shade on the outside and a lighter shade on the inside.

PHOTOFINISH WORKBOXES

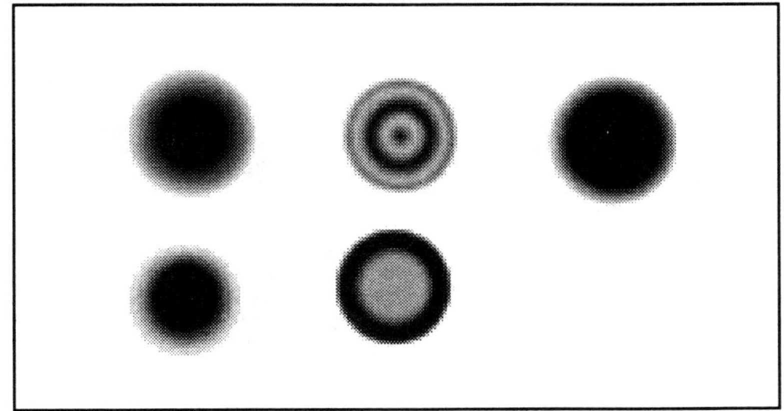

Spraycan

The Spraycan is similar to the Airbrush tool in that it sprays a random pattern of dots. However, instead of spraying a fine "mist," as the airbrush tool does, it sprays a random array of relatively coarse, discernible dots (Figure 4-14). If you hold down the mouse button without moving the mouse, the density of the dots gradually builds up. This is another tool that was greatly enhanced in PhotoFinish 3.0. In version 2.0, it is not a soft tool, and thus offers limited options for modifying its actions. Version 3.0 offers three variations:

Graffiti. This effect works as if you were actually painting on a wall with a spraycan. If you apply too much paint, it drips.

Splatter. This creates a diffused pattern of dots. It can be used to add texture to an area of a painting in which the colors are overly blended.

Two-tone. This paints in two colors: the primary and secondary. If you drag with the left mouse button, the primary color prevails. Drag with the right mouse button and the secondary color prevails.

Paint Roller

This tool allows you to quickly fill an area with the selected primary color. The paint roller icon features a thin line that represents its "hot point"—the point from which the paint is

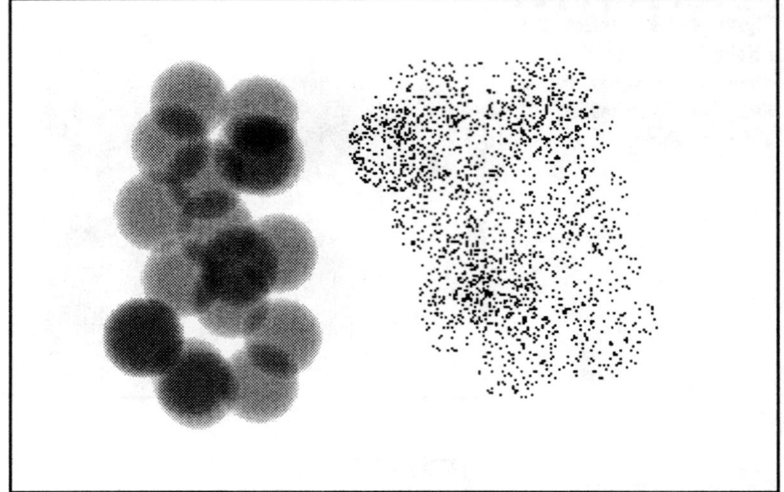

flowed. When you select the tool, you place the hot point within an enclosed area and it becomes filled with the primary color.

Be careful when using this tool. If the area in which you click is not completely enclosed by a boundary—or even if there is a small "hole" in the border—the paint "leaks" out and fills the rest of the picture. In this case, you should choose Undo, fix the boundary, and try again. If it appears that the boundary is solid, try zooming in to see if the hole is too small to be noticed at normal magnification.

When you double-click on this tool, a variation on the Color Tolerance dialog box (described earlier) comes up. This allows you to determine the range of colors that will be filled when you click with the tool. As we suggested above, you can use the Eyedropper tool to scope out the color values to be entered.

PhotoFinish 2.0 includes two related tools, the Tile Pattern Paint Roller and Gradient Paint Roller (Figure 4-15). PhotoFinish 3.0 includes the same tools as options for the basic paint roller.

The Tile Pattern Paint Roller fills the enclosed area with a pattern (Figure 4-16). The patterns themselves are Photofinish files, stored by default in the Tile subdirectory. PhotoFinish

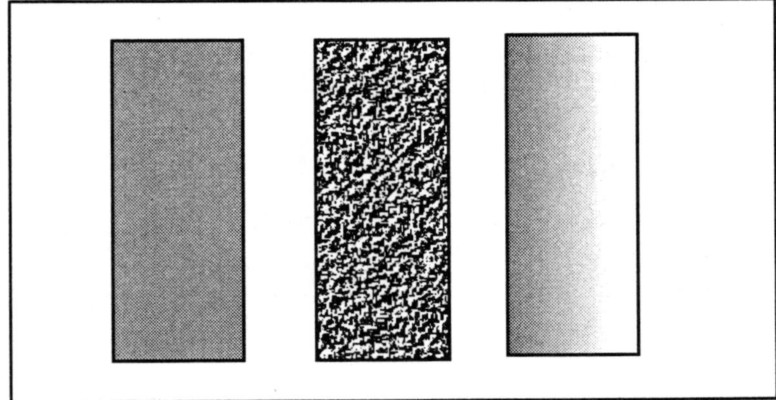

comes with some standard tile patterns, but you can add your own. To load a pattern, select the Tile Pattern Paint Roller tool and choose the Tile Pattern option from the Options menu.

The Gradient Paint roller fills the enclosed area with a gradient fill. This is a fill that features a smooth transition between the secondary color and background color. It works best in 24-bit mode and when the secondary and background colors are of the same hue.

Line

This tool is used to draw straight lines (Figure 4-17). When you hold down the Shift key, the line is constrained to horizontal, vertical, or a 45-degree angle. Normally, you draw the line simply by clicking at a certain point and then dragging the mouse. However, PhotoFinish also makes it easy to draw connected lines. To do this, draw the first line,

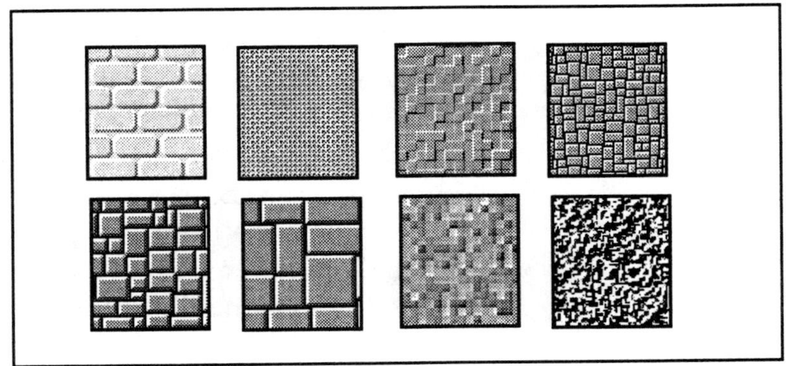

lift your finger from the mouse button, and move the cursor to where you want the second line to end. Then hold down the right mouse button, and a second line appears between the end of the first line and the point at which you clicked the right mouse button.

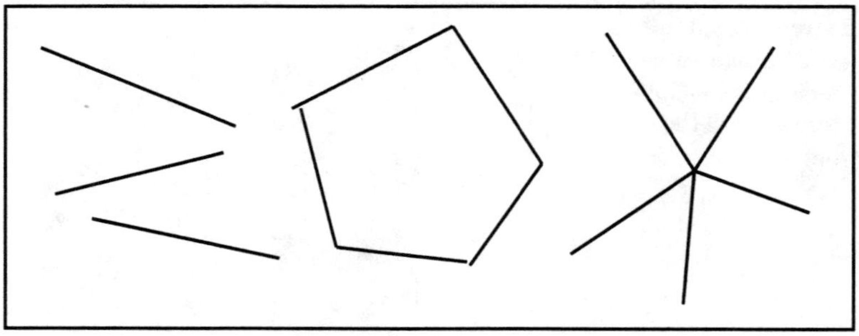

You can also draw a series of lines with the same starting point. Just draw the first line, move the cursor to where you want the second line to end, hold down the Control key, and click on the right mouse button. A second line appears between the origin point of the first line and the point at which you Control-clicked on the right mouse button.

PhotoFinish 2.0 includes a Tile Pattern Line tool that allows you to draw a line that consists of a tile pattern. In PhotoFinish 3.0 this is an option for the basic line tool.

Curve

The Curve tool, which is grouped with the Line tool, allows you to draw curves. It is quite flexible in that it allows you to determine the shape and length of the curve. When you select the tool, you first draw a straight line. You will see that two round "handles" appear within the line, and two square handles on the end (Figure 4-18).

This tool should be familiar to anyone who has used the Bezier curve feature in an illustration program like Corel Draw or Micrografx Designer. The round handles are known technically as "control points." By dragging them, you can "bend" the line to whatever shape you want.

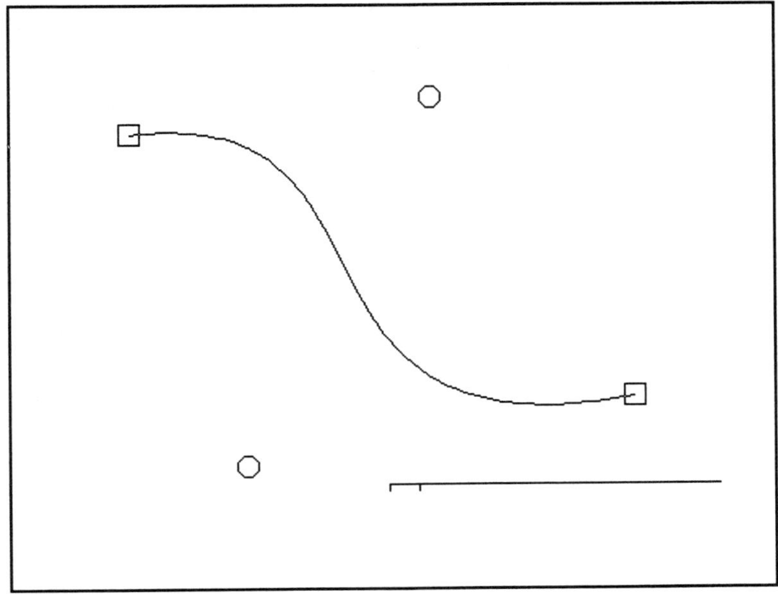

You can also drag the square handles to move the endpoints of the curve. You can draw a series of curves that are connected either end-to-end or from a common center point using the same procedure described for the line tool.

New Painting Tools

PhotoFinish 3.0 includes several new "natural media" painting tools in addition to the options included with the tools described above: Chalk, Marker, Crayon, and Color Pencil.

Chalk

This tool (Figure 4-19) creates an effect similar to drawing with chalk. It tends to draw colors a little lighter than they would otherwise appear. It also has a grainy appearance. The "Pastel" variation has a smoother effect.

If you paint while holding down the right mouse button, this tool will blend colors together as if you were smudging them with your finger. The "Powdery" option creates a smoother effect, and is one of the few painting tools for which "paper" is not an option.

Figure 4-19. Chalk options dialog box.

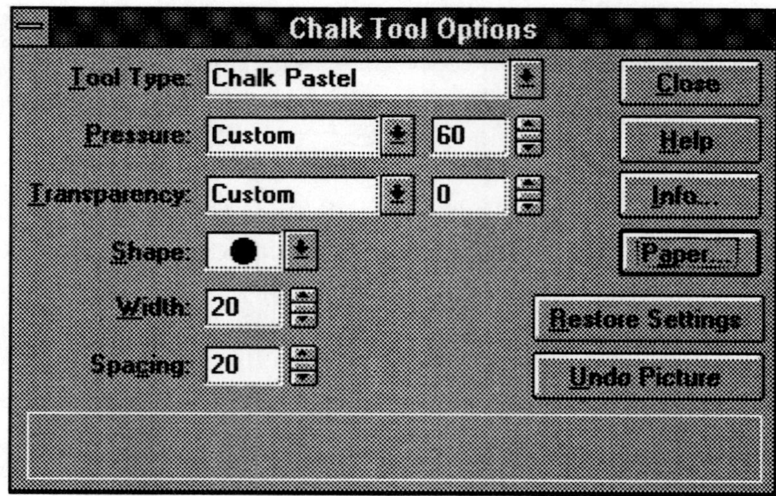

Pencil

This tool mimicks the effect of a color pencil. The "Dull" option has a higher level of transparency, while the "Sharp" option offers a more solid effect.

Marker

This tool mimicks the effect of a marker pen. The variations are "Felt Tip," "Fine Point," "Highlighter," and "Smudgy." Smudgy features a soft edge, while Highlighter has a high degree of transparency.

Crayon

This is another tool whose action should be self-evident. In general, it produces a grainy effect. The "Dull" variation is dense, with a soft edge. "Waxy" has an even softer edge. "Sharp" is thin and dense, with grainy edges. "Oil Pastel" is smooth, and eventually fades to the background color.

Shape Tools

Shape tools provide a fast way to draw regular shapes like boxes and circles. The Box, Rounded Box, Regular Polygon, and Ellipse/Circle tools are all similar. You select the tool, click at a point where you want one corner of the object to be, then drag to where you want the opposite corner to be.

The tool then creates a rectangle (Box Tool), rectangle with rounded corners (Rounded Box), a polygon, or an ellipse or circle. You can create a perfect square or circle by holding down the Shift key as you drag.

The Regular Polygon tool creates a polygon (an enclosed object with multiple sides) in which all the sides are of equal length. You can change the number of sides that will be created by double-clicking on the tool or selecting the tool and then choosing Tool Options from the Options menu. Polygons can have up to 200 sides. The Polygon tool is a little different. It allows you to create polygons with irregular sides or angles. Select the tool, move the cursor to where you want the first line to begin, click the left mouse button, then point to where you want the first line to end and the second line to begin.

When you finish the next-to-last line, double-click on the left mouse button and the polygon is completed. Holding down the shift key constrains the lines to vertical, horizontal, or 45-degree angles.

PhotoFinish 2.0 includes two sets of shape tools: hollow and filled. The hollow tools create outlines of the shapes, while the filled tools create objects that are filled with the secondary color. PhotoFinish 3.0 has just one set of tools with hollow and filled as options when you double-click on the tool.

In addition to the hollow and filled options, you can create a filled shape without a border. One use of this shape is to erase large portions of an image. Just set the secondary color to white, then draw the object. It will "white out" the areas over which you drew the object. You can do this in PhotoFinish 2.0 by setting the primary (border) color to white in addition to the secondary (fill) color.

Clone

This is one of the most powerful tools in PhotoFinish. It allows you to "clone" an area of an image elsewhere in the same image. The effect is sort of like copying a cut-out and pasting it elsewhere, except that you paint it in instead of pasting it.

Suppose you have a photograph of a person sitting at a desk. You select the tool, move the cursor over the image of the person, and click with the right mouse button. Then move to a different area of the image. Holding down the left mouse button, you paint with the clone tool.

As you move the mouse, you will see that the person sitting at the desk gets a "twin" in the new area. A set of crosshairs shows which parts of the original image are being recreated. As you move with the mouse, the crosshairs move with it. This tool is especially useful when retouching photographs. Suppose you need to fix a scratch that appears on a brick building in a scanned image.

Using the clone tool, you can draw over the scratch using the same brick pattern that appears on the side of the building. Any texture that appears in an image can be easily recreated in this manner.

In PhotoFinish 2.0, you can modify the density of the clone tool, though it is generally a good idea to keep the density at maximum (+100). Both versions allow you to modify the transparency.

By setting it to something more than zero, you can create an interesting "ghost" effect as you paint an object elsewhere in the image (Figure 4-20). The Clone tool also includes a "Rubber Stamp" option. If this option is not selected, the crosshairs continuously move over the original portion of the image as you clone it elsewhere. As a result, you recreate—or clone— the entire area covered by the crosshairs.

However, if you select "Rubber Stamp," (Figure 4-21) it is like copying only the portion of the image that appears underneath the crosshairs. That portion of the image becomes a "rubber

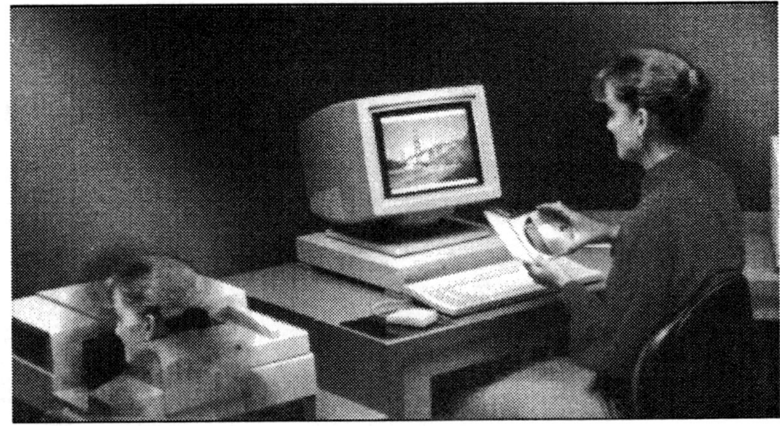

stamp," allowing you to make multiple copies of the cloned image as you click with the tool. One use of this tool would be to create a repeating pattern throughout the image.

Eraser

This tool allows you to erase portions of the image, replacing them with the background color. It appears as a square. To erase small portions of an image, you may want to use the Paintbrush instead. Just set the primary color to white (or another background color) and choose the appropriate brush shape and size. PhotoFinish gives you many more options for selecting the shape and size of the brush than for the eraser.

Color Replacer

This tool allows you to replace the primary color with the secondary color. It is useful for quickly changing the color scheme of a portion of the image. For example, if you want to change an area of red to blue, select blue as your secondary color, then paint over the red area with the Color Replacer.

This tool is especially powerful when used in conjunction with the Color Tolerance option. We noted earlier how you can use the Color Tolerance dialog box to restrict the actions of the Magic Wand or Paint Roller to a certain range of colors. With

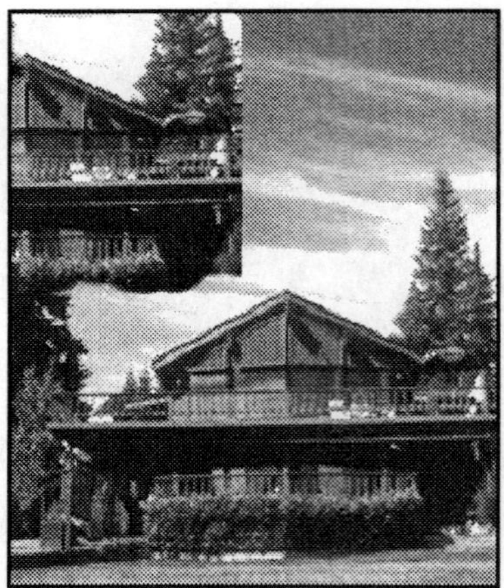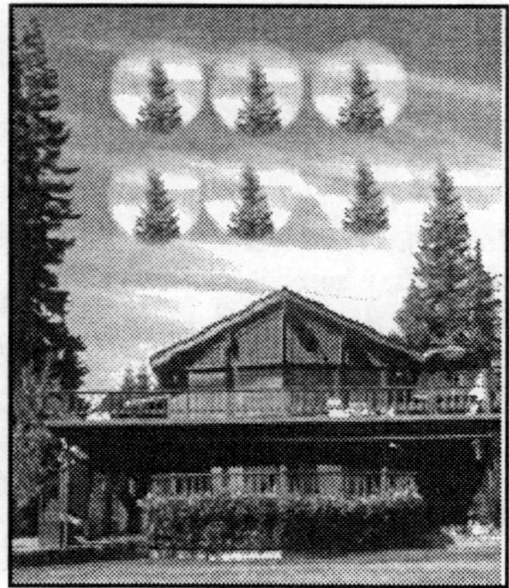

the Color Replacer, you can also limit the range of colors to be replaced.

For example, if you want to replace a certain range of reds with a shade of blue, use the Eyedropper tool to measure the color values of the red shades. Enter the lowest of these values on the negative (-) side and the highest values on the positive (+) side. When you paint over the reds with the Color Replacer, they will be converted to the background color you have selected (in this case, blue), while other colors are unchanged.

Local Undo

This is another extremely powerful tool, and one that is unique to PhotoFinish. It allows you to selectively erase the previous action, whether you applied a painting tool or pasted an object from another image. It is especially useful when creating composite images.

Even if you do a good job of selecting a cut-out to paste into a new image, there will probably be areas around the edge that you don't want pasted in. With the Local Undo tool, you can draw around the edges of the object, revealing areas of the underlying image that are otherwise obscured.

Text Tool

This tool allows you to add text to your artwork. Before you actually use the command, you must select a font in which the text will appear from the Font submenu in the Options menu. Up to four fonts can be listed here. If you want to add to or change the fonts in the list, use the More Fonts option at the bottom of the submenu.

Once you have settled on a font, select the Text tool and click where you want the text to begin. A dialog box appears in which you can type the text. The limit is about 400 characters. Be careful not to hit Enter to begin a new line of text; this will close the dialog box and return you to the artwork.

 To begin a new line of text in the dialog box, hold down the Control key and then press Enter or Return. If you have copied text to the Windows Clipboard, you can paste it into the dialog box by hitting Control-V. When you close the dialog box, the text appears within a frame. You can drag the boundaries of the frame to change the margins of the text. The text itself appears in the secondary color.

Once the text is placed on the page, it becomes a bitmapped image and cannot be edited. If you try to enlarge the image, it is possible that the text may appear to have jagged edges. If this is undesirable, you may want to create your artwork without text, then import it into an illustration or page layout program.

These programs generally include powerful features for adding text to graphic images.In PhotoFinish 3.0, text options appear in the AutoBar. This provides a quick way to modify type styles.

Retouch Tools

In addition to painting tools, PhotoFinish features several tools specifically designed for retouching photographs. Some of these tools allow you to create effects identical to those created by the Filters described in Chapter Three, or the Tune controls, which are described in Chapter Six.

The difference is that you can apply the Retouch Tools selectively simply by drawing on the canvas. If you accidentally retouch an area of the image you wanted to leave alone, you can use the Local Undo tool to restore it.

These tools are pretty much the same in versions 2.0 and 3.0 of the program. However, the approach to modifying their settings is a little different. In PhotoFinish 2.0, most of these tools bring up a palette that allows you to select the degree to which the tool will be applied.

In PhotoFinish 3.0, you can modify the effects of the tools by making selections from the AutoBar or by double-clicking on the tool to bring up a dialog box.

Contrast

This tool allows you to adjust the contrast in any portion of the image. It works in a similar manner to the contrast control on a monitor or TV set. In PhotoFinish 2.0, this tool brings up a palette that allows you to determine the level of contrast. In PhotoFinish 3.0, the degree of contrast is set in the AutoBar or by by double-clicking on the tool to bring up a dialog box.

Brighten

This tool is similar to the contrast tool, except it increases or decreases the level of brightness. It is useful in situations where a small portion of an otherwise good-looking image may be over- or underexposed. As with the Contrast Tool, you can adjust the level of brightness or darkness using a palette (version 2.0) or AutoBar/dialog box (3.0). You may be surprised at the degree of detail you can bring out in an underexposed image by painting over it with this tool.

Tint

The Tint Tool, available only with 24-bit color and gray-scale images, allows you to add a tint to an image. It is as if you held a piece of transparent colored film over the image. The tool applies the primary color as the tint. One use of this tool is to "colorize" a gray-scale image.

Blend

The Blend Tool allows you to add smoothing and softening effects to an image. The icon is a waterdrop, and the effect is similar to adding water to a watercolor painting. It is often used to soften boundaries between different areas in the image. It is equivalent to the Blend filter.

Smear

The Smear Tool, true to its name, creates a smearing effect. It can be likened to an electronic fingerpaint tool. When you paint over the image, it becomes smeared as if you were running your finger through the fingerpaint.

Smudge Spraycan

This tool, which is grouped with the Smear tool, randomly rearranges the dots in an area of the image. The effect is similar to that produced by the Diffuse filter described in Chapter Three. ZSoft recommends that you set the minimum brush width to three pixels, or else the effect will be hard to notice.

Sharpen

The Sharpen tool creates the same effect as the Sharpen filter, except it can be applied freehand. You can adjust the tool in the palette (2.0) or AutoBar/dialog box (3.0) to increase or decrease the effect.

Now that we have covered the basics of PhotoFinish, we can explore how the program will be used in real-life situations. In the next chapter, we'll discuss how images can be captured or imported for use with PhotoFinish. Then we will discuss ways to "tune," or color-correct, the images we have scanned or imported.

C HAPTER 5

Capturing Images

Most of the features in PhotoFinish are geared toward working with scanned images. But the program also offers many features that help you scan or otherwise capture images in the first place. PhotoFinish directly supports dozens of scanners, from inexpensive hand-held models to costlier flatbed devices. In addition to scanners, PhotoFinish supports several video digitizers, which are used to import images from video cameras and similar sources. PhotoFinish also supports the TWAIN software interface, a new industry standard that allows graphics programs to work with nearly any scanner. Through TWAIN, PhotoFinish can support almost any popular desktop scanner with a PC interface.

Direct support for a scanner or digitizer means that you can control the input device from within PhotoFinish without using a separate program. If you have a scanner that PhotoFinish does not support directly, you can probably use the program that came with the scanner to save image files in a format that can be read by PhotoFinish (most likely TIFF).

In addition to providing control over the scanning process, PhotoFinish includes tools that allow you to calibrate your scanner to improve the quality of images it produces. It provides automatic pre-set calibration functions if you use one of the scanners it supports directly. Because scanning is such an important aspect of PhotoFinish, we decided to devote a whole chapter to it. In this chapter, we'll look at the various options for bringing images into PhotoFinish. Along with scanners and digitizers, we'll discuss Photo CD, Eastman Kodak's technology for storing photographs on a compact disc. Though PhotoFinish does not support Photo CD directly, it can work with images imported from a Photo CD disc through Kodak's Photo CD Access software.

In addition to discussing the various options for capturing images, we'll cover PhotoFinish's scanner calibration functions. We'll also reveal how you can determine the best settings to use when scanning images.

Scanners

A scanner is a piece of computer hardware that converts images on paper or transparencies into a digital format. In recent years, prices for scanners have fallen dramatically while the technology has rapidly advanced. Today, you can purchase a highly capable color scanner for about the same price once commanded by monochrome scanners.

Scanners come in a wide variety of formats, capabilities, and price ranges. The type of scanner you should purchase depends on the kinds of images you want to capture and what you intend to do with them. If your needs are limited to line art or gray-scale images, you can get by with an inexpensive flatbed or even hand-held scanner.

If you intend to produce color images at a relatively low resolution on newsprint, there are many inexpensive color models that will meet your needs. But if you plan to produce high-quality images for a magazine or coffee table book, you may need to turn to a costlier slide or drum scanner.

Scanners used in desktop publishing systems fall into four categories: hand-held, flatbed, slide, and drum. Some older models use sheetfed or edge-fed mechanisms similar to those

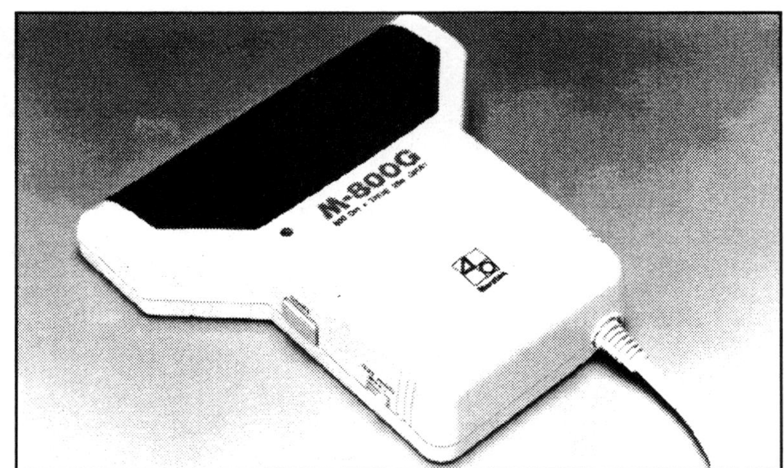

● ● ● ● ● ● ● ● ● ● ●
Figure 5-1. Hand-held scanners are the least-expensive scanning option, but they have many limitations.

in fax machines. However, few vendors continue to offer these models.

Hand-Held Scanners

In the low end of the scanner market, hand-held devices priced at $250 to $500 have carved a significant niche for themselves. These scanners have many limitations, but their low prices make them attractive to many users (Figure 5-1).

At one time, hand-held scanners were limited to scanning line-art images at a relatively low resolution. More recent models allow you to capture 24-bit color or 8-bit gray-scale images at resolutions up to 800 dpi. However, even these newer models are not recommended for situations where color image quality is a high priority.

One weakness of hand-held scanners is their limited scanning area. Some can scan images up to four or five inches in width, but others are limited to two-and-a-half inch swaths. Some software packages—including PhotoFinish—get around this by offering "stitching" features. The idea is to scan the image in separate portions and then stitch them together using the software.

Another weakness is the hand scanner's reliance on the

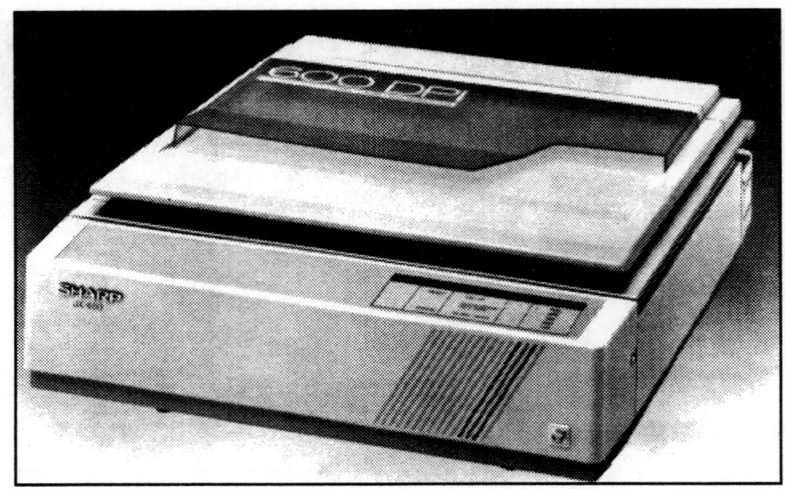

sometimes-unsteady human hand. Because it is the hand that guides the scanning mechanism, there is greater room for scanning distortions to detract from image quality.

Some companies sell plastic guides that you can use to ensure that the scanning path is straight. You can also make your own guide using wood or heavy cardboard.

Flatbed Scanners

Flatbed scanners (Figure 5-2) offer resolutions ranging from 300 to more than 1000 dpi, with most providing 300- to 400-dpi capability. Almost all flatbed scanners sold these days offer 8-bit gray-scale capability, making them suitable for capturing black-and-white photographs. However, the market is becoming dominated by flatbed models with 24-bit color capability.

Flatbed scanners resemble small photocopiers, with a removable cover and glass platen. The user places a photograph on the platen, and an array of photosensitive sensors known as charged-couple devices (CCDs) moves across the scanning area. In a gray-scale scanner, each CCD can sense up to 256 levels of gray for each dot in the image. In a color scanner, the CCDs capture images as a combination of red, green, and blue color components. They do this by scanning the image through

CAPTURING IMAGES

a series of RGB filters. Some scan the RGB in three separate passes, while others scan all three color primaries in a single pass.

Some flatbed scanners can be outfitted with accessories that allow them to scan 35mm slides and transparencies. But in most cases the images are of limited quality because of the scanner's relatively low resolution. If you want to work with slide images, your best bet is a slide scanner.

Though most flatbed scanners offer 300- or 400-dpi resolution, many advertise resolutions ranging from 600 to 800 dpi. They achieve this resolution using a method called interpolation in which the scanning software essentially makes an educated guess about the placement of dots in the image. In addition, some scanners use a hardware interpolation technique in which the scanning mechanism moves in 600- or 800-dpi increments as it scans the page. In a "true" 600- or 800-dpi scanner, there are actually 600 or 800 CCDs per inch.

Slide Scanners

Slide scanners are a popular choice for publishers of newspapers, magazines, and advertising brochures. True to their name, they capture images stored on slides and transparencies, and generally produce images superior to what a flatbed scanner can produce from a color print. One reason for this is the media on which the image is stored. Slides and transparencies are designed to transmit color information, and slide scanners thus do a much more accurate job of capturing this information.

Slide scanners offer resolutions ranging from about 1000 lines per slide to 5000 or more. Most can sense 8 to 12 bits of information per color per pixel. Several companies also manufacture transparency scanners that can handle formats up to 4 x 5 inches.

Drum Scanners

At the top of the price scale are digital drum scanners. Drum scanners essentially duplicate the features found in high-end prepress systems. The user affixes a color transparency or print to a drum that rotates inside the scanner.

Instead of using the CCDs (charge-couple devices) used in flatbed scanners, many drum scanners use PMTs (photo-multiplier tubes). The PMT technology and the precise registration of the drum allow for highly accurate scans of up to 4000 dots per inch. One advantage over transparency scanners is that the drum scanners can scan prints as well as transparencies. However, most designers prefer transparencies because they generally produce the best-looking images.

Some vendors offer interface products that allow PC users to work with the high-end scanners used in proprietary prepress systems. The scanners themselves are not desktop devices, but work with desktop computers. These interfaces are expensive, and are aimed primarily in trade shops that have already made an investment in high-end prepress systems.

Video Digitizers

A video digitizer, also known as a frame-grabber, is a hardware device that converts images from video cameras, VCRs, and other video sources into digital data. Video digitizers should not be confused with digitizing tablets, which allow users to draw images using an electronic stylus and tablet.

Digitizers are usually sold in the form of a board installed in the PC; the video source is connected to a jack in the board by means of a standard cable. PhotoFinish directly supports several video digitizer products. Once an image is captured with a digitizer, it is identical to an image captured by a scanner.

A digitizer offers the ability to produce instant halftone images, since you don't have to bother with photo processing. But low-cost digitizers are generally limited in the quality of the images they can produce. They are also unsuitable for capturing images on paper. Digitizers that offer high-resolution image capture are quite expensive.

Digital Cameras

A digital camera is a still camera that captures and stores images in digital form. Because the image is captured as a digital file, you don't need a video digitizer to import it into the computer system. The first company to offer such a product was Dycam, which called its camera the Dycam Model 1. The camera could store up to 32 images, each measuring 376 pixels by 240 pixels with 256 levels of gray. After capturing the image, the Dycam camera passed it through a serial port to the PC. The camera included an electronic flash unit.

Photo CD

Eastman Kodak's Photo CD system is one of the most exciting new technologies to hit the electronic publishing market. The technology allows for storage of photographic images on a special form of compact disc. When your film is processed at a photo lab, you can have your images stored on the Photo CD disc as an alternative to conventional processing. Each disc can store up to 100 images.

These images can be viewed in one of two ways. Using a Photo CD player or CD-I player, such as Philips' Imagination Machine, you can view the images on a standard television set. But you can also import the images into a computer system using a CD-ROM XA drive. These inexpensive drives, which are fast becoming standard equipment in computer systems, are capable of reading data from any CD-ROM disc, including Photo CD.

The XA in CD-ROM XA refers to "extended architecture," a variation on the CD-ROM drive that has enhanced capabilities. One of these is "multisession" capability, meaning the drive can read data that has been written to the CD after the first set of data has been recorded. This is important with Photo CD discs, because you can have images stored on the disc in multiple trips to the photo lab. Without a CD-ROM XA drive, you are limited to importing only the first set of images recorded on the disc.

PhotoFinish does not support Photo CD directly. However, Kodak offers an inexpensive software package called Photo CD Access that allows Windows users to import images from the Photo CD and save them in one of several standard file formats, including TIFF. Once the image is stored in TIFF format, you can then bring it into PhotoFinish for manipulation. It is likely that future versions of PhotoFinish will directly support Photo CD.

Scanner Control in PhotoFinish

If you have a scanner or digitizer that PhotoFinish supports directly, you can capture images using commands available in the Scan menu. Otherwise, you need to use the software sold with the scanner to capture the image. You can then save the image in TIFF or PCX format and bring it into PhotoFinish. You will probably find that the scanner control software sold with your scanner is similar to the scanner controls in PhotoFinish.

The scanner controls in PhotoFinish (Figure 5-3) allow you to determine the brightness, contrast, scanning area, scale factors,

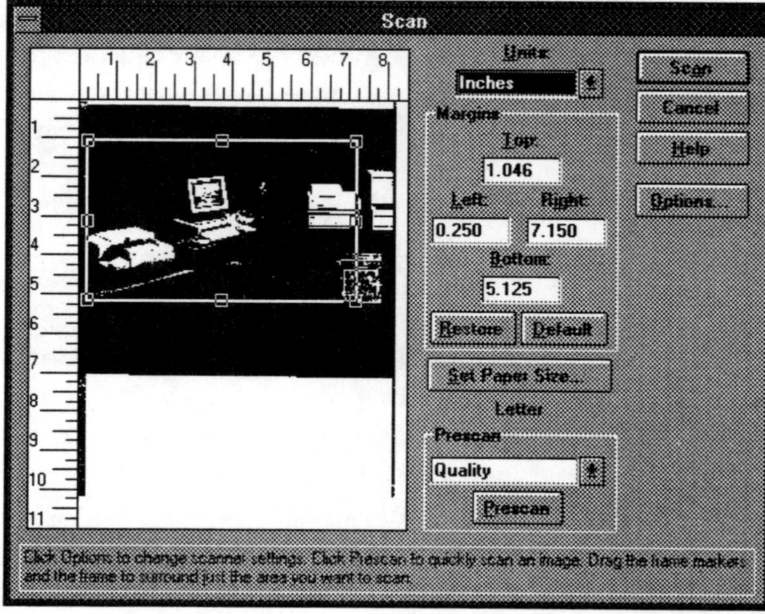

Figure 5-3. The Scan dialog box.

and resolution of the scanned image. They are accessed through the PhotoFinish Scan menu. In addition to controlling the scan, you can also have PhotoFinish perform automatic image-enhancement operations to the image.

When you install PhotoFinish, the program asks you to specify which scanner or digitizer you plan to use. If your scanner is supported by PhotoFinish, it installs a scanner "driver" that allows use of the device with the program. When you access the scanning functions, they are already set up for your particular scanner.

Most of the PhotoFinish scan controls are accessed through a Scan dialog box. The program actually has three Scan dialog boxes, one for flatbed scanners, one for hand-held scanners, and one for digitizers. All three dialog boxes have a similar look. All consist of a Scan Area box on the left and scanner or digitizer controls on the right.

If you are using a flatbed scanner or digitizer, the first step in scanning most images is to perform a pre-scan. This is a quick scan that places a low-resolution version of the image in the Scan Area box. It is useful for two reasons: you can quickly see if the image is crooked or otherwise needs to be moved, and it allows you to select only the portion of the image you will actually need, thus reducing file size.

If you are using a flatbed scanner, you have two pre-scan options: draft and quality. Draft scans the image in black-and-white, while quality scans it in color. Keep in mind that the pre-scan options will have no effect on the final image. You can pre-scan an image in black-and-white and then perform the final scan in color.

If you are using a digitizer, you have two additional options: Single and Multiple. If you choose Single, the digitizer will pre-scan the scene once and display it in the Scan Area box. If you choose Multiple, the digitizer will perform a continuous scan of the scene, showing changes as they occur. The

Pre-Scan button becomes a Stop button. Click on it to stop the pre-scan.

After you perform the prescan, the image is surrounded by a frame with eight handles that allow you to determine the area to be scanned. You do this by dragging on the handles until the frame surrounds the desired portion of the image. Once you are satisfied with the scanning area, you click on the Scan (flatbed) or Capture (digitizer) button in the upper right-hand corner of the dialog box to perform the final scan.

Other controls in the dialog box allow you to enter values to determine the scanning area instead of dragging on the frame handles. However, most users find it easier to drag the handles and perform the image cropping visually. As you move the handles, you will notice that these values change automatically to reflect the new boundaries.

One difference between the Digitizer and Flatbed scanner dialog boxes is that the former includes brightness and contrast controls underneath the Scan Area box. If you are doing a Multiple Pre-Scan, you can see the effects of these controls before you perform the final image capture. Brightness and contrast controls for flatbed scanners are accessed by clicking on the Options button (see below).

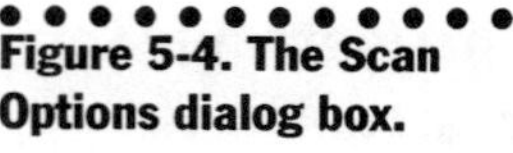

Figure 5-4. The Scan Options dialog box.

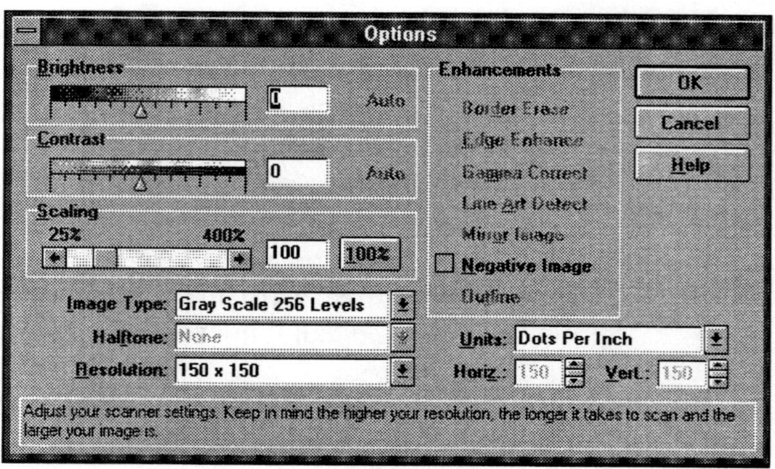

The Hand Scanner dialog box is different from the other two dialog boxes in that it does not include a pre-scan option. However, it does include a Feedback option that allows you to see the image as it is being scanned.

Whatever kind of scanner you are using, additional scanning controls are accessed by clicking on the Options button. This brings up the Options dialog box (Figure 5-4). PhotoFinish includes a single Options dialog box for all three types of image-capture devices. Any feature not available to your particular device is dimmed out.

Depending on the kind of scanner you are using, this dialog box allows you to set brightness, contrast, scaling factors, image type, and resolution. You can also have PhotoFinish perform one of several image enhancement operations. Some of these operations, such as mirror image, negative image, and outline, duplicate functions that can be applied to the image through other PhotoFinish menu options.

Brightness and Contrast

The brightness and contrast settings in PhotoFinish are similar to the brightness and contrast controls on a television set. You can set brightness and contrast using the slider controls, or enter a number from -100 to +100. The higher the number, the higher the level of brightness or contrast. You can click in the Auto option to have the scanner apply its default brightness or contrast settings. As a rule, most scanners tend to darken images, so you will usually want to increase brightness.

Scaling Factors

This control allows you to determine the degree to which the image is enlarged or reduced as it is scanned. Though you can also reduce or enlarge an image after it is scanned, it is best to do it at this point if you know what size you want the image.

Again, you have the option of using a slider control or

Figure 5-5. The Halftone option uses a dithering technique, which converts gray levels (right) into a series of dots (left).

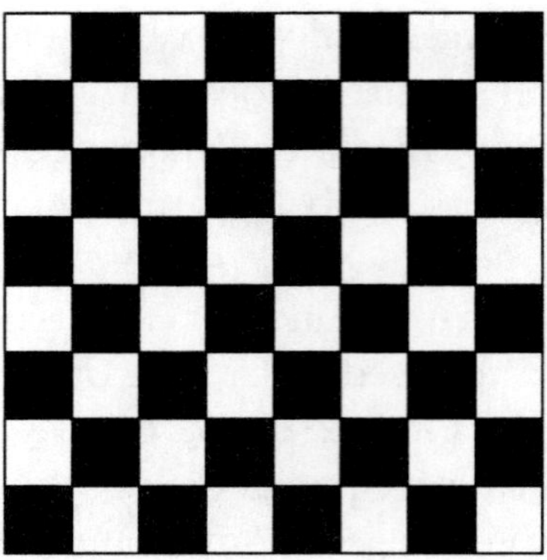

entering a value. Values are entered in percentage terms. For example, to double the size of the image, you would enter 200 percent. To reduce it to one-fourth its original size, enter 25 percent.

For reasons we shall see below, the scaling factor is related to the resolution of the image. In fact, there is no real difference, in terms of the final image, between scale factor and resolution. An image scanned at 150-dpi at a 100-percent scale factor is identical to an image scanned at 300-dpi with a 50-percent scale factor.

Image Type

This allows you to determine the kind of image you want scanned. You can choose from black-and-white, gray-scale, or color image types.

Halftone

This option applies if you want to scan an image in black and white. A halftone, as we saw in an earlier chapter, is an image composed of tiny dots. Dark areas have relatively large dots, and light areas have relatively small dots. When your image is ultimately printed, it will probably be produced in the form of a halftone. However, in almost all cases, you will want to scan the image in gray-scale or color mode and ignore this option.

The Halftone option in the Options dialog box allows you to create a halftone as the image is scanned. In technical terms, images created in this way are known as dithered images (Figure 5-5). Instead of sensing the image as a series of colors or gray shades, the software converts it into a series of dots, larger dots in dark areas and smaller dots in light areas.

There are two problems with dithered images. One is that the image becomes locked into this dot pattern. If you try to enlarge or reduce it later, a moire pattern will result. The other problem is that the image has a limited resolution. Even if your scanner is capable of 300- or 400-dpi resolution, the resolution of the halftone (known as the "screen frequency") will be much less than this. The reason is that the dots seen by the scanner are all the same size.

To create a halftone, the software groups the scanned dots into clusters known as halftone "cells." These cells are equivalent to the dots in a halftone. The cells themselves are a fixed size. Cells in light areas will have a relatively small number of dots, with the rest of the cell composed of white space. Cells in dark areas will be filled with a greater number of dots. If the halftone pattern has large cells, it creates the illusion of a halftone with many gray shades.

However, the image also appears to be coarse, with a low screen frequency. A halftone pattern with smaller cells will have a higher screen frequency, but cannot simulate as many gray shades.

The Halftone option allows you to determine just how these cells will be set up. If you choose "None," the software will create a simple black-and-white image with no halftone screen.

The other options, which are listed in the PhotoFinish user guide, allow you to determine how many dots will compose each halftone cell, and the pattern of dots within the cell. Coarse Fatting, for example, allows for a relatively high number of gray shades at a cost in resolution.

The Bayer pattern, on the other hand, allows for fewer gray shades but higher resolution. You can also choose an Error Diffusion option, which offers a more random distribution of dots without a halftone cell pattern.

One use of the Halftone option is if your scanner lacks gray-scale capability. You can scan the image as a halftone, then use the Remove Moire filter described in Chapter Three to remove the screen pattern and convert it to a true gray-scale image. The quality won't be the same as if you scanned the image on a gray-scale scanner, but it's better than dithering.

Resolution

This option allows you to set the resolution of the scan. It will display only the options available for your scanner. As noted above, the resolution is associated with the scale factor. In the next section, we will explore just how these settings are related and offer tips for determining the best resolution and scale factors to use.

Determining Resolution

A common mistake made by scanner users is scanning an image at the maximum resolution no matter what they plan to do with it. This may be advisable if you are working with a pure black-and-white image, because you want to get the crispest image possible. However, if you are scanning a gray-scale or color image, you will end up wasting a lot of file space.

We noted above that resolution and scale factor are associated with each other. In fact, there is really no difference between the two. What is important is to create a file that includes all of the image data you need and no more. To determine how much data you need, you have to know something about how the image will be printed. The assumption here is that you plan to produce the image on a PostScript imagesetter, but the same technique applies no matter what output device you plan to use. There is a relatively simple formula that will help you determine the size of the image file you want to create:

Screen frequency^2 x image size x 1 1/2 or 2

In other words, take the screen frequency of the final halftone, square it (multiply it by itself), multiply this by the number of square inches in the image, and then multiply this by one-and-a-half or two. You perform the last calculation to give yourself a "fudge" factor—a little more data than you will actually need.

This formula assumes that you are working with a gray-scale image. If you are working with a color image instead of gray-scale, multiply everything by three to account for the extra image data. Suppose you want to create a halftone with a screen frequency of 100 lines per inch at a size of 2 x 3 inches. The square of 100—in other words, the number of halftone dots in a square inch—is 10,000. An image measuring 2 x 3 inches has a total of six square inches. Multiply six by 10,000 and you get 60,000 halftone dots in the entire image.

Multiply 60,000 by 1.5 and you get 90,000, or roughly 90 kilobytes. Multiply it by 2 and you get 120,000. Since the "fudge factor" is a matter of preference, you can shoot for an image file with 90 or 120 kilobytes of data. We use a similar formula to figure out how much image data will be created by our scan:

Image size x scanning resolution^2 x scale factor

Let's go back to the Options dialog box. Suppose the image we are scanning measures 4 x 6 inches. That's a total of 24 square inches. Suppose we have set the resolution at 150 dpi; 150 squared is 22,500. Multiply the image size by 22,500 and you get 540,000, or 540 kilobytes.

We are shooting for about 90 to 120 kilobytes, so we need to reduce the image size. Using our handy calculator, we find that 90 is about 17 percent of 540. Therefore, we set the scale factor at 17 percent. If we want to go for 120 kilobytes, the scale factor should be about 22 percent. (Again, multiply everything by three if you are dealing with color images.)

In theory, you could also set an arbitrary scale factor, say 50 percent, and figure out the scanning resolution you would need to get the same result. However the math is a little more complicated and most scanners have limited resolution options anyway.

Therefore, it is usually best to set the resolution at an arbitrary figure—usually about 100 or 150 dpi—then use the scale factor to adjust the size of the image file. Some scanning programs make this easy by showing you the file size that will be created by the scan based on your settings. Unfortunately, PhotoFinish is not one of these programs. However, the math is easy enough to do once you know the formula.

AutoScan

PhotoFinish includes an AutoScan function, accessed through the Scan menu, that will automatically scan your image. This function automatically straightens crooked images, removes moire patterns, and adjusts brightness and contrast. You can click on the Options button in the AutoScan dialog box to adjust the automatic scanning settings. In PhotoFinish 3.0, the AutoScan option is available from the Ribbon bar in addition to the Scan menu for quicker access.

Stitch

This option, which is most often used with hand scanners, allows you to add an image to an existing image in the active window. It is useful because hand scanners have a limited image area. You can scan the image in separate "chunks," then use the Stitch option to combine them into a single image within PhotoFinish. When you access this function, the new image is added to the right of the existing image. The new image is surrounded by a selection marquee, similar to what you would see if you used a cutout. You can then move the new image into alignment with the first image. The first image is automatically resized to accommodate the additional image.

Calibration Functions

One of the most useful features in PhotoFinish is its scanner calibration function. This function uses files containing what are known as "transfer" or "compensation" curves to automatically modify images, taking into account the scanner's known characteristics when capturing images. No scanner is absolutely accurate when scanning an image. A 50-percent gray or color shade, for example, may come in at 60 or 70 percent. A 10-percent shade may come in as pure white.

To compensate for this, you can apply a calibration "map" that adjusts gray or color values in the image to correct the inaccuracy. For example, if a scanner consistently scans a 50-percent gray shade at 60 percent, the calibration map automatically lightens the mid-tones of the image to bring them closer to 50 percent. PhotoFinish includes pre-set calibration maps for the scanners it supports. You can load these maps and apply them as the image is scanned. However, it is a good idea to modify the maps even if your scanner is supported, because there can be variations among different scanners of the same make and model.

Calibrating your scanner is a very simple operation. PhotoFinish includes a calibration card, also known as a "target." The target includes gray shades and colors with values that are known to the program. To calibrate the scanner, you first select the Calibrate option from the Scan menu and choose one of the preset maps. If your scanner is not listed, try to select one that is similar.

Next, click on Options, and a new series of options appears at the bottom of the dialog box. Click on New to create a new calibration file and give it a name. It will be based on the calibration file you selected previously. Place the target in the scanner and click on the Recalibrate option. PhotoFinish scans the target and compares the scanned values with the known values for the target. It then creates a compensation map that adjusts future scans accordingly. The calibration map can also be automatically modified using the Recalibrate option.

The process of creating the compensation map is transparent to you, the user. However, if you choose, you can use the Edit option to modify the curve manually. It is probably not necessary to do this, and if you don't know what you're doing, it can be downright dangerous to the quality of your images. But it can be done.

In the next chapter, we'll look at ways to create and modify your own compensation maps. We'll cover the functions that PhotoFinish provides for calibrating your monitor and output device. We'll also explore other options for improving the look of your images.

CHAPTER 6

Enhancing Images

Once an image is scanned, PhotoFinish offers many options for enhancing it. Most of these options are found in the Image menu. In this chapter, we will discuss the characteristics that separate a good-looking image from a not-so-good-looking one. We'll explore the functions in PhotoFinish that provide information about the contents of our images. And we'll show you how to use those functions to make any necessary enhancements to the image.

Our Goal

Our goal in using the image enhancement functions in PhotoFinish is to produce images that will look good in print or wherever else they end up. We are not interested in producing fancy special effects or composite photos that invite lawsuits or forgery charges. We just want an image that looks as good as, or even better than, the original.

What are some of the characteristics we look for in a photograph? First, the colors must conform with our experience of reality. The shade of green we see on the maple leaves should be close to the shade of green we see on the leaves in our back yard. People, unless they come from Mars, should not have a greenish tint. Second, the photograph should have a reasonable balance between shadows (dark areas), highlights (light areas), and mid-tones. Third, the photograph should not be over- or under-exposed. Once an image is scanned into a computer system, it often has trouble matching up to these high standards we have established for it. It may be a little strong in the red, giving a fiery cast to the image. It might be perfect in the foreground, but underexposed in the background.

Most of the color correction features in PhotoFinish are found in the Tune submenu of the Image menu. At this point, a comment on the differences between versions 2.0 and 3.0 is in order. Just as Version 3.0 adds Samples options to the Filters and Special Effects submenus, it also adds them to the Tune submenu.

You can use the Samples command to see examples of all Tune options. In addition, each of the Tune options provides visual samples of various settings in the form of thumbnail images. This can be a tremendous time-saver: instead of previewing the effects of various settings, you can see them all in one place and choose the one that appears to be the best.

The image processing tools in PhotoFinish offer useful functions for identifying and correcting these problems. PhotoFinish also offers powerful tools for calibrating the hardware devices used in your color publishing system. We finished the last chapter with a discussion of scanner calibration. We will begin this chapter by covering monitor and printer calibration.

Monitor Calibration

Before we use PhotoFinish's image processing tools, it might be a good idea to try out its monitor calibration function. Just as PhotoFinish offers functions for calibrating your scanner, it also allows you to calibrate your monitor. Though your monitor will never do a perfect job of accurately displaying the image, calibrating it will get it as close as possible.

Some manufacturers of color display systems offer calibration products that modify the hardware used to display images. The calibration tools in PhotoFinish are different. Instead of modifying the hardware, PhotoFinish includes functions that help it measure the color display characteristics of the monitor. This information is stored in a monitor calibration file. When the calibration file is loaded, PhotoFinish automatically adjusts the colors in the image so they will display as accurately as possible on the screen. Several calibration files are included with the program, but you can also create your own, or modify the ones included in the program. Doing this is as easy as clicking on a series of boxes displayed by the program.

The calibration file contains a curve known as a gamma or compensation curve. The curve is a way of modifying the values that represent colors. We learned earlier that all colors and all gray shades can be represented as a series of numbers. A gray-scale image contains dots that can be any one of 256 shades of gray. Therefore, each dot can be represented as a value between 0 and 256.

In a 24-bit color image, each dot can be one of 256 shades of red, green, and blue (or cyan, yellow, and magenta). Imagine three pieces of film, one red, one green, and one yellow. Each piece of film can be one of 256 shades of its respective color. When you put those pieces of film together and shine a light through them, they can represent any color within the RGB spectrum depending on which of the 256 shades you chose for each film.

The problem with color displays (and scanners and printers) is that each represents color a little differently. Once PhotoFinish knows how your monitor represents colors, it can use the gamma curve in the calibration file to modify the RGB values for the most accurate possible display.

Monitor calibration functions are accessed by selecting Monitor Calibration from the Display menu. A dialog box appears that lists several popular monitors (Figure 6-1). You can pick from the list, or click on Options to create a new calibration file for your monitor. When you click on Options, a series of buttons appears at the bottom of the dialog box. To create a New

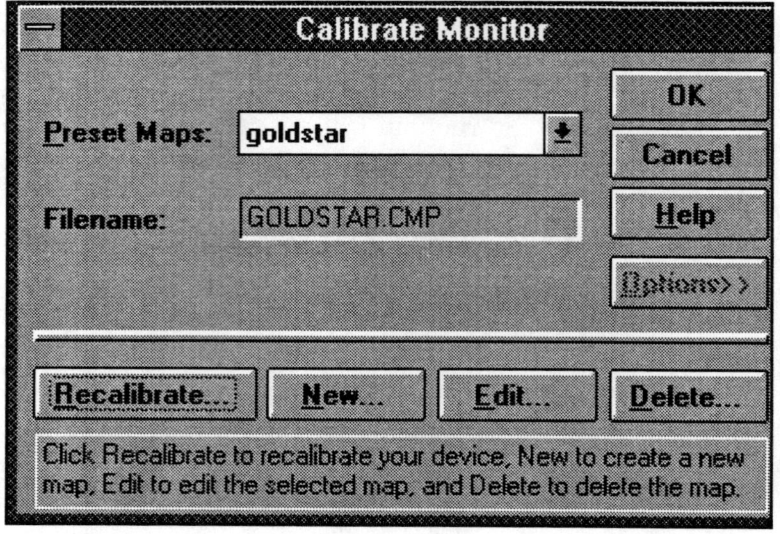

Figure 6-1. The Calibrate Monitor dialog box. The selections at the bottom of the dialog box appear when you click on the Options button.

calibration curve, click on New. When you do this, the program will ask you to enter a file name for the calibration curve. It is a good idea to use the make or model of your monitor as the file name (unless you like to give your monitors names like Fred or Wilma).

PhotoFinish automatically copies the previously selected monitor calibration to the new file. Your next step is to

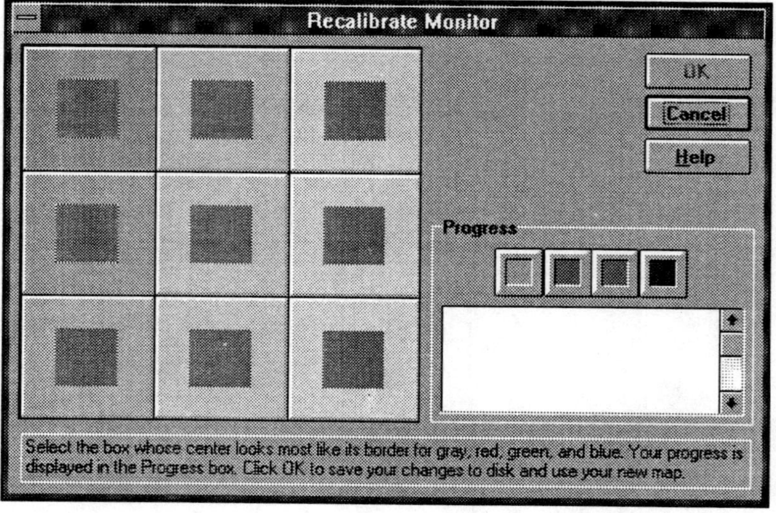

Figure 6-2. To calibrate your monitor, you click on a series of squares.

recalibrate the curve so it works with your monitor. To do this, click on Recalibrate.

The program now displays a dialog box containing a series of nine squares with smaller squares in the middle (Figure 6-2). You click on the square in which the smaller square most closely matches the square that surrounds it. Keep doing this until the program has created a series of gammas for gray, red, green, and blue. These gammas are listed in a scrollable list to the lower right of the dialog box. When the process is finished, the program will tell you that the calibration has been successfully completed. You can then close the dialog box. The calibration file you have just created can be loaded and modified at any time thereafter.

You can also edit the calibration curve directly by clicking on Edit. A graph appears showing the relationship between the base color values (the color values stored for the image) and the color values that should be displayed on the monitor (Figure 6-3). This graph is similar to the compensation maps that appear when you use the Tune Color/Gray Map option in the Image menu. Compensation maps will be explained later

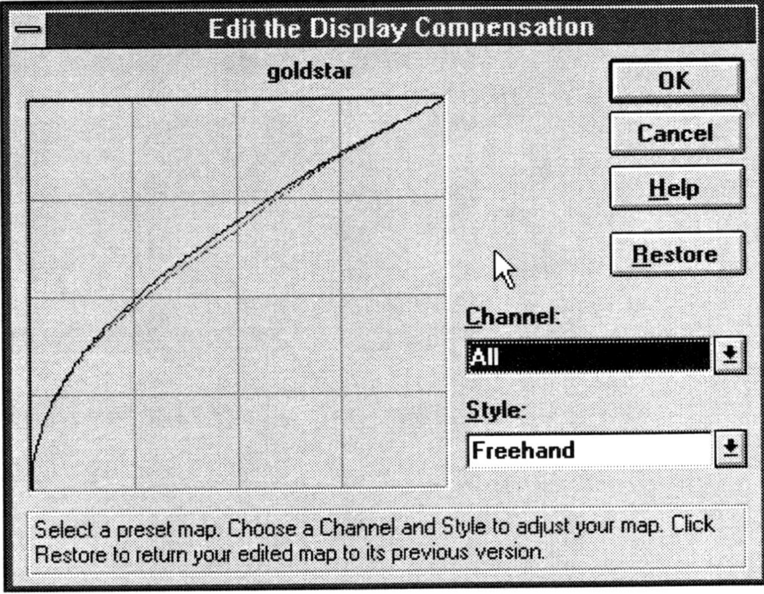

Figure 6-3. A compensation curve created by the Photo-Finish Calibrate Monitor function. You can modify the calibration by altering the line.

in this chapter. Suffice it to say that you should probably forego altering the monitor calibration curve once it has been created or recalibrated. Be forewarned that a monitor will never display an image exactly as it will be printed. Monitors display colors in the form of transmissive light, while printed colors represent reflective light. However, PhotoFinish will adjust images as best it can to compensate for the color display characteristics of the monitor.

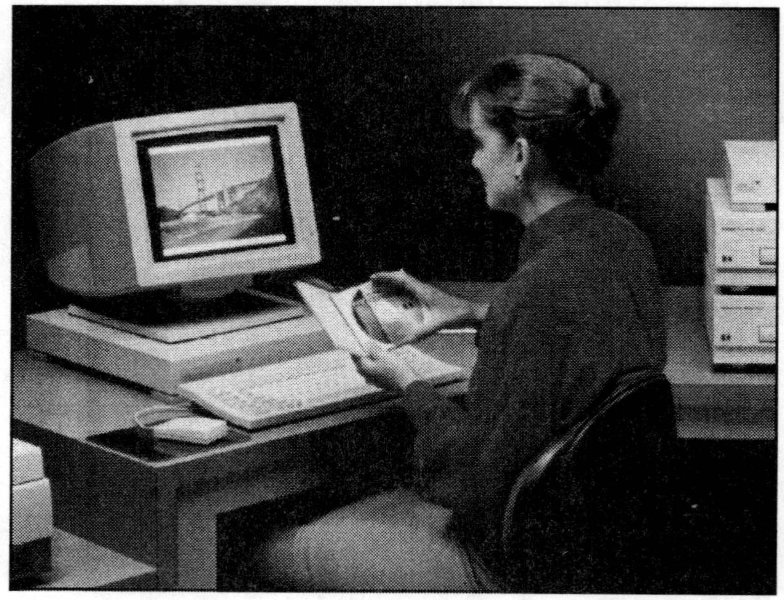

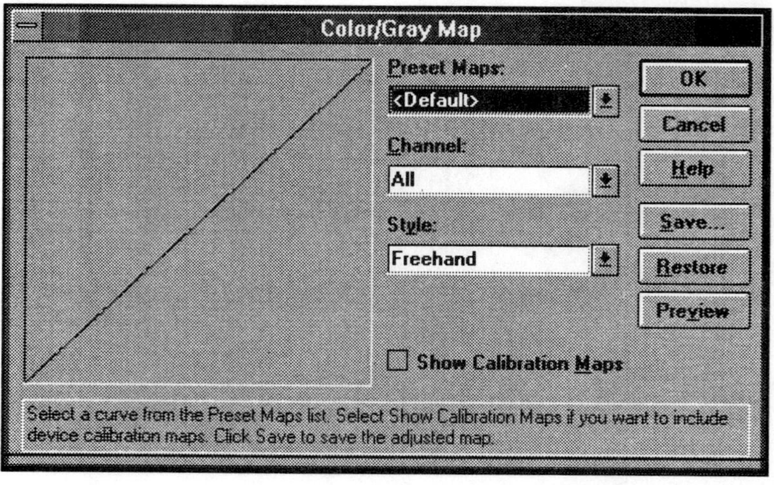

Printer Calibration

Printer calibration works in a similar way to monitor calibration. Here, you use the Calibrate Printer option from the File menu. PhotoFinish includes generic compensation maps for popular printers, but you can fine tune the program for your specific output device.

PhotoFinish includes a file called CALIBRTE.PCX that contains

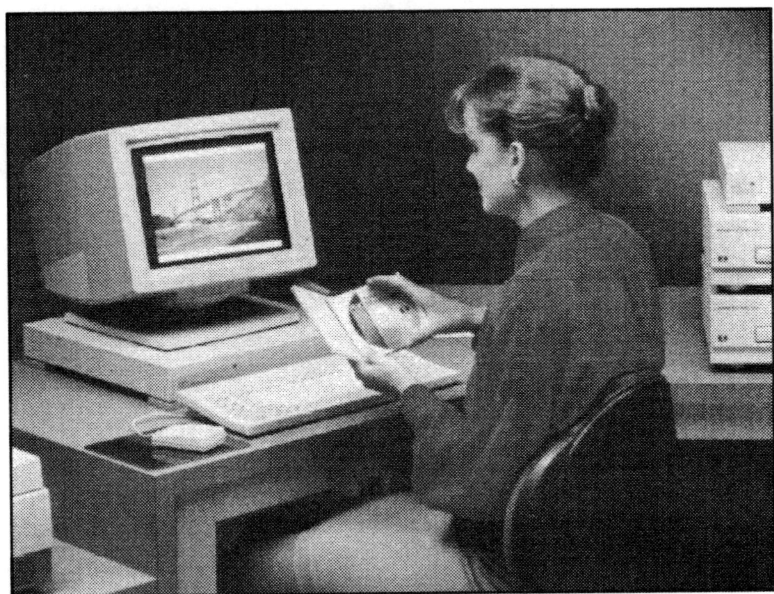

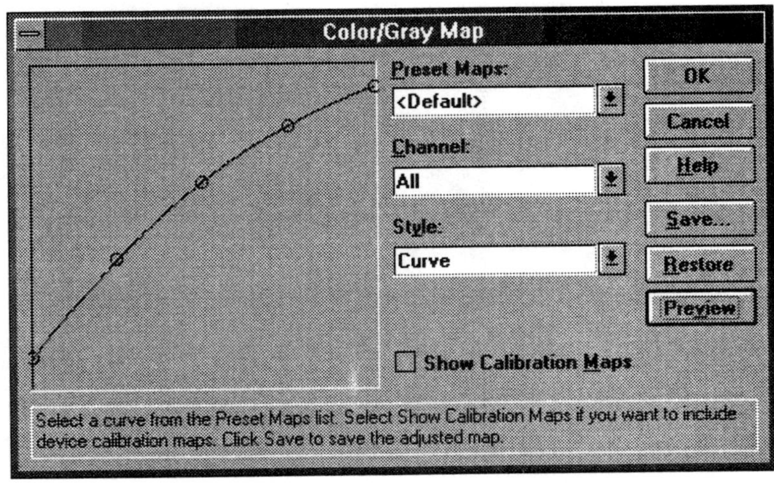

a standardized image. When you select the Calibrate Printer option, PhotoFinish prints this file on your printer, then prompts you to scan it. Information from the scan is used to build a calibration curve that is similar to the monitor calibration curve. As with the monitor calibration curve, the printer curve can be saved, loaded, recalibrated, and edited.

Modifying Compensation Maps

The calibration options for the scanner, monitor, and printer are transparent to the user. But you can also modify images using your own compensation maps. These maps are created using the Tune Color/Gray Map option (Figures 6-4 through 6-7).

As noted above, a compensation map is a graph. It appears as a box with a line running more-or-less from the upper right to the lower left. The x-axis (along the bottom) represents the values in the original image. The y-axis (along the left) represents the values in the new image.

The bottom of the y-axis and left side of the x-axis represent black or maximum color density. The top of the y-axis and right side of the x-axis represent white or minimum color density.

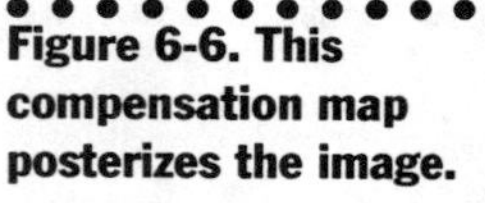

Figure 6-6. This compensation map posterizes the image.

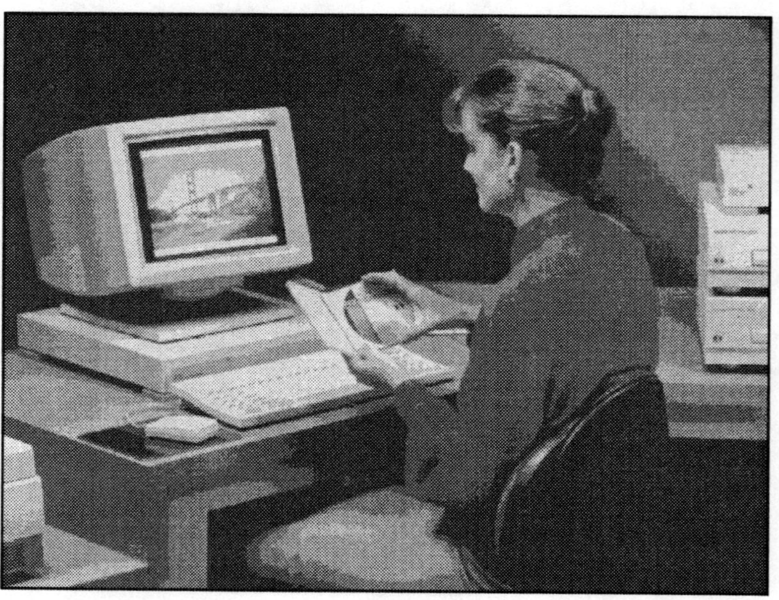

ENHANCING IMAGES

The line represents the relationship between the colors or gray values in the original image and those in the new image. You can apply the compensation map to a gray-scale image or a color image. You can apply the map to all colors at once, or to the three individual color "channels": red, green, and blue. To keep things simple, we'll describe how the map works with a gray-scale image.

In a normal image, the line runs from the upper right to lower

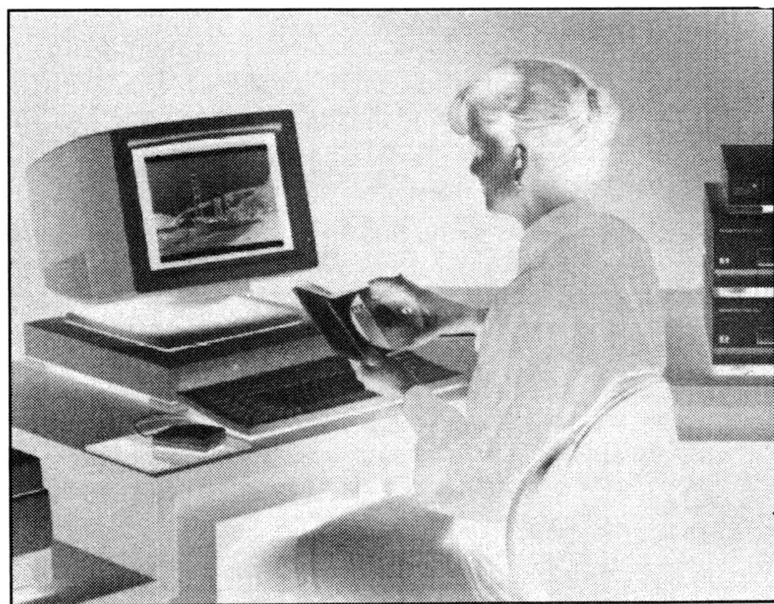

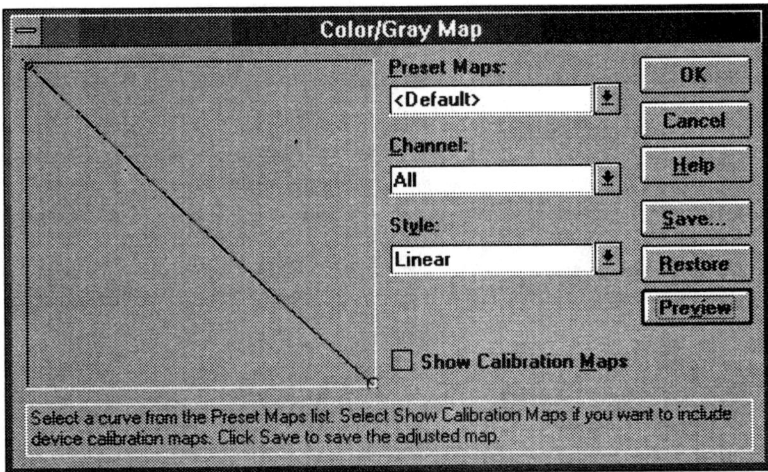

left. This means there is a one-to-one correspondence between the gray shades in both images. A 90-percent gray shade (near the bottom left of the graph) in the original image is also a 90-percent gray shade in the new image. Now suppose we raise the line a little. That 90-percent gray shade in the original image is now an 80-percent gray shade in the new image.

Now let's get more radical. We'll run the line from the upper left to the lower right. The 90 percent gray shade in the original image becomes a 10 percent gray shade in the new image. All of the gray values are reversed, and we end up with a negative version of the image. PhotoFinish offers three options for moving the line. The curve option allows you to move one of several handles that appear on the line. You can move the handles up, down, left, or right. The Freehand option allows you to redraw the entire line. The Linear option allows you to drag either end of the line, which has the effect of increasing or decreasing the level of brightness.

Considering that PhotoFinish includes calibration features for scanners, printers, and monitors, it may seem redundant to have a similar feature in the Image menu. But there are many cases when you may want to apply compensation map independent of the calibration features. For example, if your scanner is not directly supported by PhotoFinish, you can create a compensation map that will calibrate the unit (albeit not as easily as the built-in calibration function).

You can also use a compensation map to create special effects. For example, you can create an effect known as "solarization" by reversing the gray or color values in the middle of the compensation map while leaving the rest alone.

You can also create your own posterization effect similar to that produced by the Posterization filter. Another use of the compensation map is to correct individual color channels. For example, an image may appear to have a reddish cast. To correct this, choose Tune Color/Gray Map from the Image menu, select the Red channel, and lighten it up.

Finally, you can use the compensation map to account for differences among printing presses and paper stocks. This is important if you plan to produce color separations of your images on a PostScript imagesetter. When printing on highly absorbent uncoated papers like newsprint, dots tend to spread more than they do on coated stocks or less absorbent uncoated stocks. This phenomenon is known as "dot gain." The result is that the image appears darker than it should. You can correct this by lightening the image with a compensation map.

You can do the same thing by adjusting the brightness of the image using the Tune Brightness and Contrast option in the Image menu. But the advantage of the compensation map is that you can save different maps for different kinds of presses or paper stocks and then load them as needed.

Using The Histogram

There are many ways that we can determine how well an image will look in print. One way is simply to look at it on a monitor. Though this is not an entirely accurate predictor of how the image will look, you can tell if there are any obvious problems such as severely under- or over-exposed areas.

However, PhotoFinish offers other ways to obtain information about an image. One of the most useful is the histogram. A histogram is a graph that shows the distribution of gray shades or colors in an image. It consists of thin vertical lines arranged along a horizontal axis. Each point on the axis corresponds to a color or gray value moving from white or low density on the left to black or high density on the right. The length of the vertical line tells you how many pixels in the image match that particular gray or color value. A long line means there are a lot of pixels with that value, while a short line means there are few pixels of that value.

The histogram thus gives you a quick way of telling how gray or color values are distributed in an image. An overexposed image will show many long lines clustered toward the right side of the histogram. A high contrast image will show two separate clusters of long lines, one at each end of the graph.

Ideally, the lines in a histogram should be distributed along the entire graph in a gradual bell-shaped curve. If too many lines are clustered in a small portion of the graph, it is likely that the picture will be lacking in detail. Of course, this is not necessarily true with all images. A shot of a starry sky, for example, will show a lot of long lines clustered toward the dark side of the spectrum with a smaller number of shorter lines closer to the light side. But if the shot is supposed to show a wide range of colors or gray shades, and the histogram indicates there are not, you may have a problem with the photo.

The histogram in PhotoFinish is accessed through the Tune Equalize option in the Image menu. If the graph indicates that there are serious problems with the image, you may want to rescan it with different brightness and contrast settings. To do this, click on the Cancel button and return to the Scan menu. Otherwise, you can get a better distribution of gray or color values using the Equalize function.

PhotoFinish allows you to make separate equalization settings for the low (dark), middle, or high (white) values in the histogram. Do this by dragging the respective arrows for these settings. Any shades to the left of the Low arrow will become black, and shades to the right of the High arrow will be white. The Mid arrow redistributes the shades in between. It is a good idea to use the Preview function to see the effects of any changes (it will also help you to understand how the function works).

Other Tuning Functions

So far, we have discussed two powerful options under the Image Tune menu, Tune Color/Gray Map and Tune Equalize. However, PhotoFinish includes three other Tune functions that are worth mentioning.

Brightness/Contrast

This function adjusts the brightness and contrast of an image. It is similar to the brightness and contrast controls on a TV set. Use the brightness control to lighten or darken an image. Use the contrast control to bring out detail in an otherwise muddy image. You can apply the filter to the entire image or a selected portion. You can also use the Brightness and Contrast retouch tools to perform the same operations freehand.

As noted above, PhotoFinish 3.0 allows you to view thumbnail samples of various brightness and contrast settings when you call up the dialog box.

Hue and Saturation

Use this function to modify the hue and saturation in an image. By adjusting the hue, you can create wholesale shifts in the colors in the image, turning, for example, green elements into red. You can enter values from 0 to 360, with each value corresponding to a different hue. This is similar to using the HSL model in the PhotoFinish Color Picker.

You can also adjust the saturation, or intensity of the colors. Enter a value from -1.00 (minimum saturation) to +1.00 (maximum). Values from -.50 to +.50 produce the best results.

Negative

Tune Negative offers a quick and easy way to turn your image into a negative.

Now that we have covered the image enhancement features in PhotoFinish, we are ready to look at some real-world examples of how to use the program.

CHAPTER 7

Modifying Images

Now that we've explored the many features in PhotoFinish, it is time to put our knowledge to use. In this chapter, we'll look at some sample applications that might be performed with PhotoFinish, with step-by-step instructions along the way.

The PhotoFinish documentation includes a Tutorials manual with its own step-by-step exercises using images included with the package. In addition to studying the examples in this book, we suggest that you try experimenting with the Tutorial examples on your own.

The examples used here will put many of the program's functions to work. Hopefully, what you learn from going through these examples will help you in your own use of PhotoFinish.

Because many of the steps in these examples use the color manipulation functions in PhotoFinish, we have included a color section to show the images as realistically as possible. Images found in the color section are identified with the letter "C," as in "Figure C-1."

Getting Out From Behind The Eight-Ball

Your copy of PhotoFinish came with one or more handy diskettes containing clip art. The images are stored in the JPEG image compression format discussed in Chapter Two. Along with the image library is a contact sheet showing thumbnail versions of each picture.

Image Number 1006 (Figure C-1) shows that eternal symbol of bad luck, an eight ball.

Since no one wants to be behind the eight ball, as it were, we'll use the color manipulation functions of PhotoFinish to turn it into a yellow one-ball.

Getting Started

The first step is to open the file.

1. Locate the diskette labeled "PhotoLibrary 1" and load it into your disk drive.

2. Go to File Open. The Open File dialog box comes up.

3. Use the Drives box to locate the drive (most likely Drive B) in which you placed the diskette.

4. Open the file "1006.jpg."

PhotoFinish will automatically decompress the file as it is opened. When the image comes up on screen, it is a good idea to first save it to your hard disk. But before you do this, you may want to crop the image to save the amount of memory it requires for processing. Remember, the smaller the image, the less memory it consumes.

To crop and save the image:

1. Locate the Box Selection tool in the Toolbox and click on it.

2. Draw a marquee around the portion of the image you want to save. To do this, start in one corner of the box you want to draw and drag toward the opposite corner as you hold down

the mouse button. Draw the marquee so that it surrounds the eight ball, leaving some of the pool table around it. A box will appear around your selection.

3. Go to the Edit menu and click on "Crop." A cropped version of the image—including only the portion you selected—will appear in a new, untitled window.

4. Go to the File menu and select Save. Save the image under a new name (we used "EIGHT-BL.TIF"). The file extension is added automatically when you select the file type.

5. When the file is saved, you can get rid of the original. You could keep it on the screen in the background, but it will only clutter things up while consuming extra memory. Select the window containing the original (either click on the window or select it from the Window menu), then select File Close. Now you are ready to go to work.

Tools and Strategies

We will primarily use the following tools to change the color of the ball: The Eyedropper, Color Replacer, Paintbrush, and Text. We will also use the Color Tolerance and Palette Range of Colors commands, both of which are found in the Options menu.

Our general strategy here is to use the Color Replacer and Paintbrush tools to change the color of the ball from black to yellow. We will also use the text tool to replace the "8" with a "1." Just to make things interesting, we will attempt to duplicate the shading in the ball, in addition to changing the color, to make it look more realistic.

The ball appears to be black, but the black is actually blacker in some areas than others. To see this for yourself, select the Eyedropper tool, and *without* holding down the mouse button, drag it over the eight ball (Figure 7-1).

If you look at the status bar at the bottom left of the screen, you will see that PhotoFinish provides the RGB values for any area over which you drag the Eyedropper.

This assumes that you are in RGB, as opposed to HLS, mode (more on that later). If the status bar is giving you HLS values, choose the Palette Range of Colors command from the Options menu and choose "RGB" as the color model.

You will see a series of relatively low values, ranging from zero to about 50. You will also see that the values for red, green, and blue stay close to each other. Remember from Chapter One that black is made from equal amounts of RGB.

We will use these values to perform a little magic with the Color Replacer. If you recall from Chapter Four, the Color Replacer replaces the secondary color with the primary color. Using the Color Tolerance command, we will define a relatively wide range of blacks to replace. Then, using the Eyedropper tool, we will select narrower ranges of black to replace.

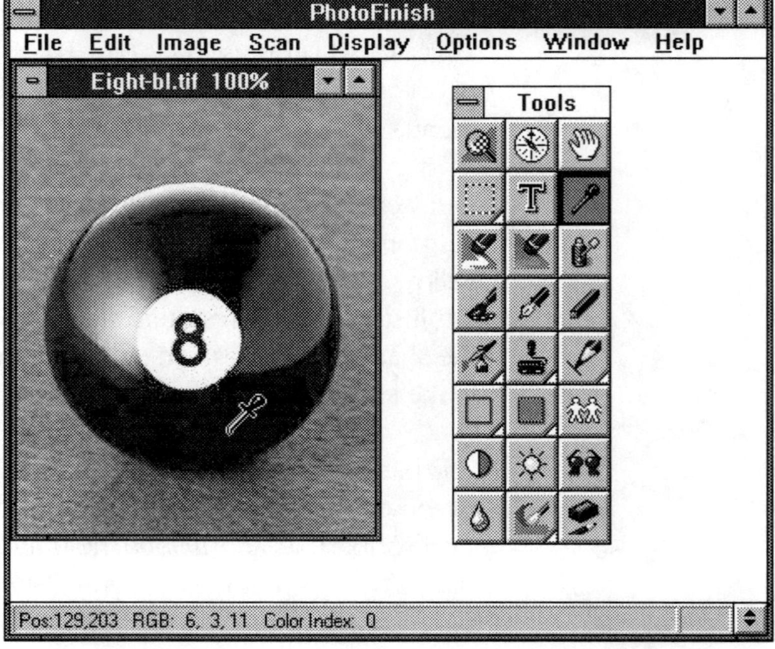

Figure 7-1. By dragging the Eyedropper tool over the image, you can see the RGB or HLS values of individual pixels.

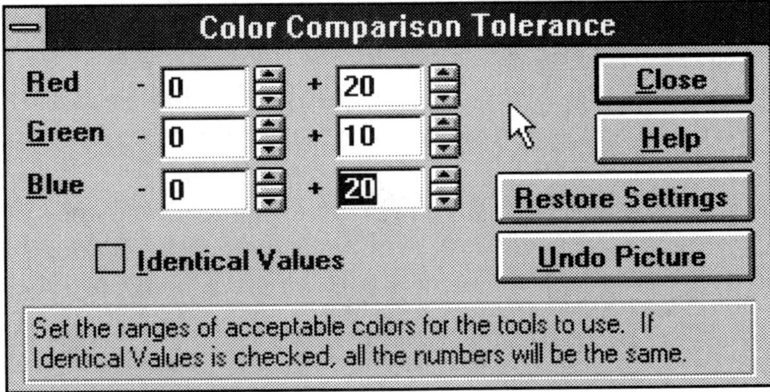

Figure 7-2. The Color Comparison Tolerance dialog box allows you to set the RGB values to be affected by several tools, including the Color Replacer. The values entered here cover the darkest shades in the image. These are the shades that will be replaced.

Replacing Colors

The Color Tolerance command works with the Color Replacer, Magic Wand, and all three paint roller tools. It defines the range of colors that will be affected by these tools as expressed in RGB values. We saw above that the Eyedropper tool gives us information about the RGB values in the eight ball. We will use this information with the Color Tolerance command:

1. Without holding the mouse button, drag the Eyedropper tool over the eight ball and record the RGB values for the darkest areas. They range up to about 20 Red, 10 Green, and 20 Blue. We will use these values to begin replacing black with yellow.

2. Select Color Tolerance from the Options menu (Figure 7-2). Be sure that identical values is not clicked. On the left are the negative values: the lowest values for the colors you want to replace. Set each of these at zero, which would represent the blackest black. The positive numbers represent the upper range (on a scale of zero to 256). Set 20 as the upper range for Red, 10 for Green, and 20 for Blue. Because there is a lot of contrast between the eight ball and the background green felt, the numbers don't have to be exact, but R20, G10, and B20 should work well.

3. Select black as the primary color. Do this by clicking with the left mouse button on a black square in the Palette. The top square in the Color Selection Box on the left should be black.

4. Select a deep shade of yellow from the Palette.

5. Select the Color Replacer tool. Use the Width & Shape workbox to set the brush width big (you can go up to 40).

6. Paint over the eight ball with the Color Replacer tool (Figure C-2). You will see that the darkest portions of the eight ball become yellow, leaving the remainder of the image unaffected. It doesn't matter if you accidentally paint outside the ball; the values you set in the Color Tolerance box prevent any colors outside the defined RGB range from being affected.

You should be able to paint over much of the ball in this manner. If you set the Color Tolerance higher, you will paint over a greater range of black shades in the image. But now let's get fancy.

We want to replace the differing shades of black with the equivalent shades of yellow. To do this, we first want to change our Palette to give us a wide range of yellow shades.

We will also switch from RGB mode to HLS. Why? First, we use RGB because the Color Tolerance command accepts only RGB values. But from now on, we will use the Eyedropper tool to select the color to be replaced. The advantage of the Color Tolerance command is that we can define a broad range of RGB values to change in one fell swoop. But if we are replacing many different shades of a color in an operation, the Color Tolerance command can be cumbersome. You'd be constantly figuring out RGB values and entering them in the Color Tolerance box. The Eyedropper tool, on the other hand, lets us pick colors much more quickly. The disadvantage is that we can only pick a narrow range of colors.

Another reason to change from RGB to HLS is that the HLS model is more intuitive visually. When you drag the RGB slider controls in one of the Palette dialog boxes, you probably have little idea of what color will result unless you look at it. With the HLS model, you can pretty much predict what will happen

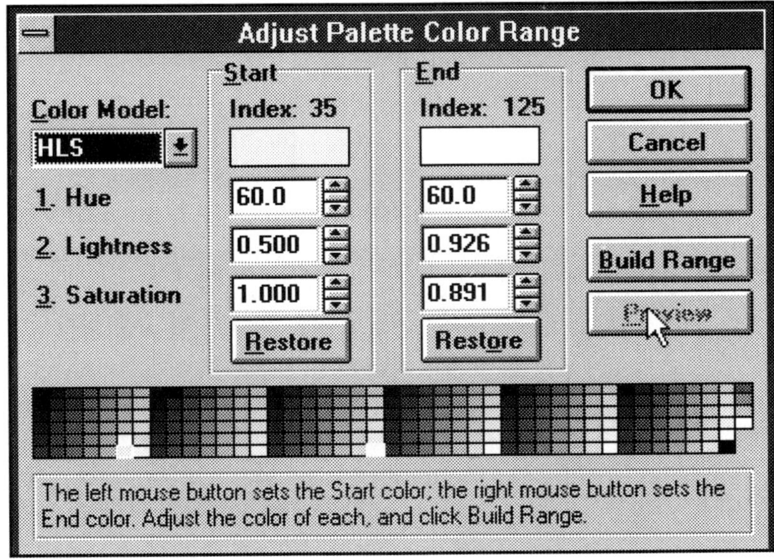

when you adjust the hue, saturation, and lightness: hue changes the color, saturation the purity of the color, and lightness the intensity of the color. It's no accident that you have hue and brightness controls on your color TV set as opposed to RGB controls.

Selecting Shades

What we want to do now is select a range of yellow shades corresponding to the range of black shades in the eight ball. We want to replace a particular black shade with its yellow equivalent.

If you wanted to be exact about things, you could measure the precise HLS values in the eight ball and replace them with the identical lightness and saturation values, with yellow as the hue. You could also use a spoon to fill your bathtub with water. Yes, replacing exact lightness and saturation values is more exact, but it is also more time-consuming. Which isn't to say that there might not be certain projects where you would want to take this approach.

But first let's pick some yellow shades:

1. Choose Palette Range of Colors from the Options menu (Figure 7-3).

2. Choose HLS as the color model.

3. Click the left mouse button on the shade of yellow you selected earlier. This is your start color. The Hue value should be around 60 (assuming you chose yellow).

4. Click the right mouse button on another shade of yellow to the right of the first shade. Allow enough space for a sufficient range of yellow shades. The exact shade you pick doesn't matter because you can always change it with the slider controls. Just be sure that the Hue number is the same, or close (either that or choose any color and change its Hue value to 60).

5. Use the slider controls to change the lightness and saturation settings for the End color. Slide the lightness control to a point where the color is almost white. Then make the color slightly less saturated. The End color will be used for the lightest black portion of the eight ball—the part that's reflecting a little glare.

6. Click on Build Range. PhotoFinish will replace the colors between the Start and End colors with a smooth transition of yellow shades. When you close the dialog box, you will see that your Palette now includes the new range of yellows.

Finishing Up

Now we're ready to finish replacing the black shades.

1. Select the Eyedropper tool.

2. Go to Tool Options in the Options menu. You can choose to have the Eyedropper pick a single pixel, an array of 3-by-3 pixels, or an array of 5-by-5 pixels. We'll start with 5-by-5, but as the areas of black get smaller and smaller, we'll move to 3-by-3 then single pixel. In 5-by-5 mode, the Eyedropper will

select the average shade of the five pixels surrounding where you click.

3. Find an area of black in the eight ball that was not affected by the Color Replacer when you used it earlier. Click on the left mouse button to select that as your primary color. Remember that the primary color appears in the upper square in the color selection box. Don't make the mistake of selecting a secondary color when you want a primary and vice-versa.

4. Select an equivalent shade of yellow for your secondary color. Click with the right mouse button on the desired shade in the Palette. This color should appear inside the hollow square on the right of the Color Selection box.

5. Select the Color Replacer tool and continue painting over the eight ball until it no longer has any effect.

6. Select another black shade with the Eyedropper tool as your primary color and another yellow shade as your secondary color, and continue as above. It is a good idea to move from relatively dark shades to relatively light ones for both black and yellow.

7. You will notice that some spots of black remain no matter how many times you paint over them. You can fill these in using the Paintbrush tool (Figure C-3). It is a good idea to zoom in at this point, because the Paintbrush tool does not constrain itself to certain colors the way the Color Replacer does.

You can use the Zoom command in the Display menu, but the Zoom tool in the Toolbox is a bit more productive because you can zoom in on the specific area where you are working (just click with the zoom tool in the center of where you want it to zoom).

8. If you make a mistake and paint outside the area of the ball (or over a light shade with a dark shade), use the Local Undo tool to paint away the mistake. If your paint "spills" onto the

green felt, you can also use the Clone tool to replicate the felt on top of the paint.

The advantage of the Clone tool is that it reproduces complex patterns in addition to simple colors. At this point, it may be a good idea to use the Blend filter to smoothe the transition between the various shades of yellow.

1. Use the Elliptical Selection tool to draw a marquee around the ball. Start from the center of the ball, and hold down the Shift key to constrain the marquee to a circle.

2. Choose Filter Blend from the Image menu. Try a medium effect, but you can use the preview top experiment with other settings.

3. As an alternative, you can try using the Blend retouch tool. When you select the tool, a new Palette appears replacing the familiar color Palette. This allows you to determine the degree of blending. This tool can be especially useful around the edges of the ball.

Finally, we need to change the 8 to a 1. First we will erase the "8," then we will replace it with a "1."

1. If you want to go the "quick and dirty" route, use the Eyedropper tool to select the white shade inside the circle as the primary color (left mouse button). Use the paint brush to paint out the "8."

2. If you want to be more precise, use the Clone tool to replicate the exact pattern of white in the circle and paint out the "8." One warning: if you paint over an area with the Clone tool to change it, you must click on the Clone tool again if you want to replicate the newly painted area. Otherwise, the Clone tool will replicate the area that was originally under the new coat of paint.

3. Select Fonts from the Options menu.

4. Choose the font and type size you'd like to use. If it does not appear in the font list, click on More Fonts to select it. In most cases, selecting a type size will require some trial and error. We found that 10-point worked well in this case.

5. Select the color for the new number by clicking in the Palette with the right mouse button (the text color is considered the secondary color).

6. Select the Text tool and click anywhere in the image. The Text box appears.

7. Type in the new number.

8. When you close the box, the text appears inside a cut-out box. You can then move it into place by dragging with the mouse (Figure C-4).

As long as text remains a cut-out, you can change its color by clicking in the Palette with the right mouse button. If you deselect the text by clicking outside the cut-out (but inside the image), the text will be "glued" into place.

That should do it! Zoom out, and you will see that you are no longer behind the eight ball.

Cleaning Up the Goodyear Blimp

For our next piece of magic, we will clean up a color photo of the Goodyear blimp. Then we will paste the blimp into a photograph of a trade show and make it appear that the blimp is flying inside the convention center.

First we scan the blimp using the scanning functions in PhotoFinish. However, we have not calibrated our scanner, so the blimp comes in too dark, especially underneath. So our first job is to brighten it up.

1. Select the Brightness Retouch tool. In PhotoFinish 2.0, the

Brightness palette comes up. In PhotoFinish 3.0, we can select the same options using the AutoBar.

2. We begin painting on the underside of the blimp. If nothing happens, we can raise the brightness level. If we are raising the brightness level too much, we can Undo the action of the retouch tool and try again at a lower brightness level. (The Undo command is an important ally in our quest to create a good-looking photo because it allows us to experiment. If the action we have taken cannot be undone, we can always close the image without saving it and open the original.)

Suddenly we can see details in the blimp that were not visible before (Figure 7-4).

Creating A Composite

Now we want to cut and paste the blimp into the photo of the convention center. But first, we need to remove the anchor lines tying the blimp to the ground (after all, we want it to fly inside the convention center).

1. First we select the Clone tool.

2. We zoom in and click on the grid pattern on the bottom of the blimp with the right mouse button. The idea is to replicate the pattern over the lines so they disappear. We click on the right mouse button as many times as necessary to replicate the correct pattern. Keep in mind that the program replicates the pattern that was present since you last selected the tool.

If you paint out the anchor lines, then click on that area of the blimp with the right mouse button, you will end up replicating the anchor lines. Thus it is a good idea to go back to the toolbox and click on the Clone tool whenever you are happy with your progress.

3. Then we prepare the blimp for cutting and pasting. We use

the Lasso tool to draw a marquee around the blimp. We don't have to be precise; we can leave some space around the edges of the blimp.

4. Next, we use the Copy command in the Edit menu to copy the image of the blimp to the Windows clipboard.

5. We close the file, then select Open from the File menu. Instead of selecting a file, we click on Clipboard. PhotoFinish opens a new file and pastes in the blimp. Here we can perform any other image editing operations that are needed, such as removing any additional wires.

6. We need to reduce the size of the blimp to manageable proportions. We choose the rectangular selection tool from the toolbox and draw a marquee around the blimp.

7. We select Transform Resize from the Image menu. We enter a size about one-half the current width. By clicking on Proportional Resize, we will maintain the ratio between height and width (known as the "aspect ratio). When we change the width, the height automatically changes. Alternatively, we can select Free Resize and reduce the blimp by dragging on the handles that appear around it.

Now we are ready for our final piece of magic.

Figure 7-4. The Brightness tool reveals details in the image we didn't see before.

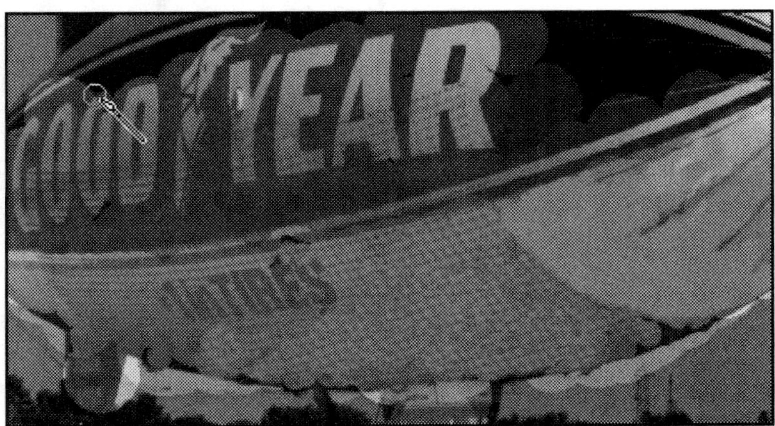

1. We choose the Lasso selection tool and once again draw a marquee around the edges of the blimp.

2. We choose the Copy command from the Edit menu.

3. Now we open the file called SHOW.TIF. This image, which we scanned previously, depicts the floor of a trade show as seen from the ceiling.

4. We use the Paste command from the Edit menu to paste the contents of the Clipboard into the scene. The blimp now appears to be flying above the show—and inside the convention hall.

5. We move the blimp toward the upper left by dragging. We then click outside the selected area, which pastes the blimp into place.

We can see that the blimp is a little "rough around the edges," with small portions of the previous image surrounding its borders.

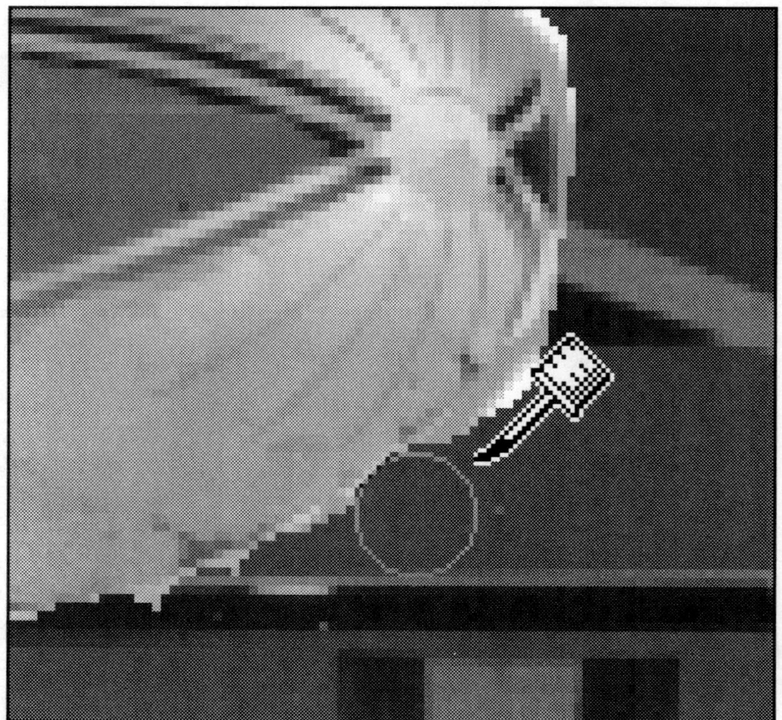

Figure 7-5. We use the Local Undo tool to paint around the edges of the blimp.

1. We zoom in on the blimp using the Zoom command in the display menu. We'll first try it at 200 percent.

2. Next, we select the Local Undo tool. Very carefully, we paint around the edges of the blimp (Figure 7-5). As we do so, the scene that was obscured by the blimp is revealed. We have successfully flown the blimp into the convention center. If we want, we can use the Clone tool to give the blimp a companion.

The final result is a scene that defies reality: a blimp flying inside the convention center. Take that, Steven Spielberg and George Lucas!

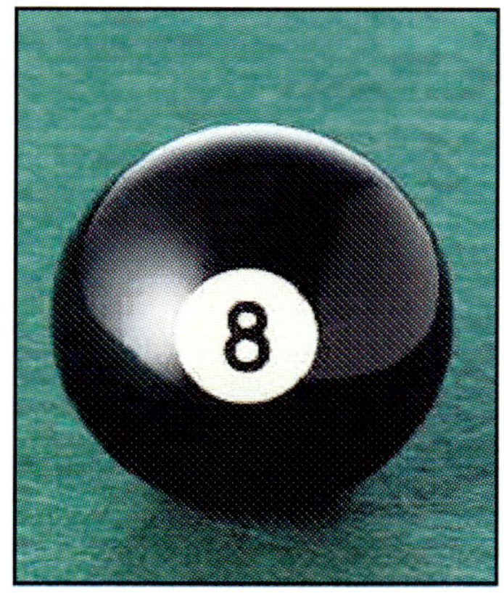
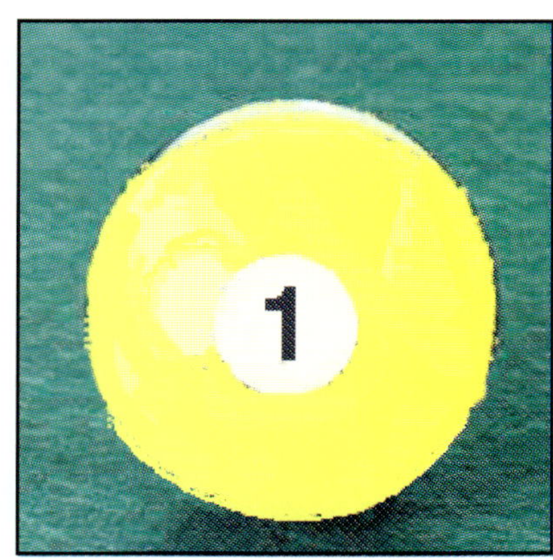

Figure C-1. Our goal is to turn an eight ball into a one ball.

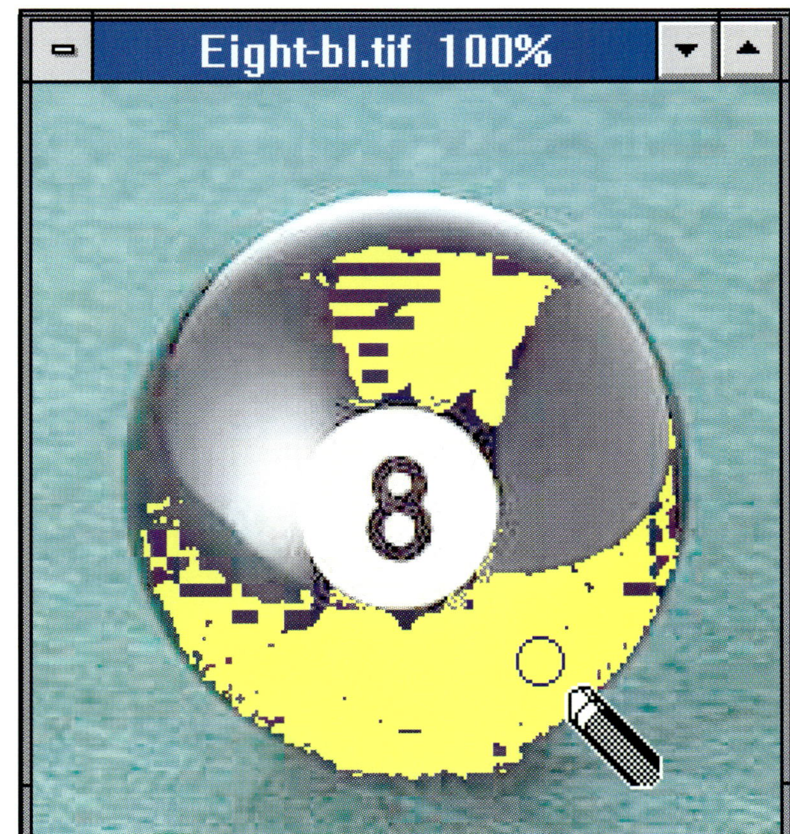

Figure C-2. We use the Color Replacer tool to replace black with yellow.

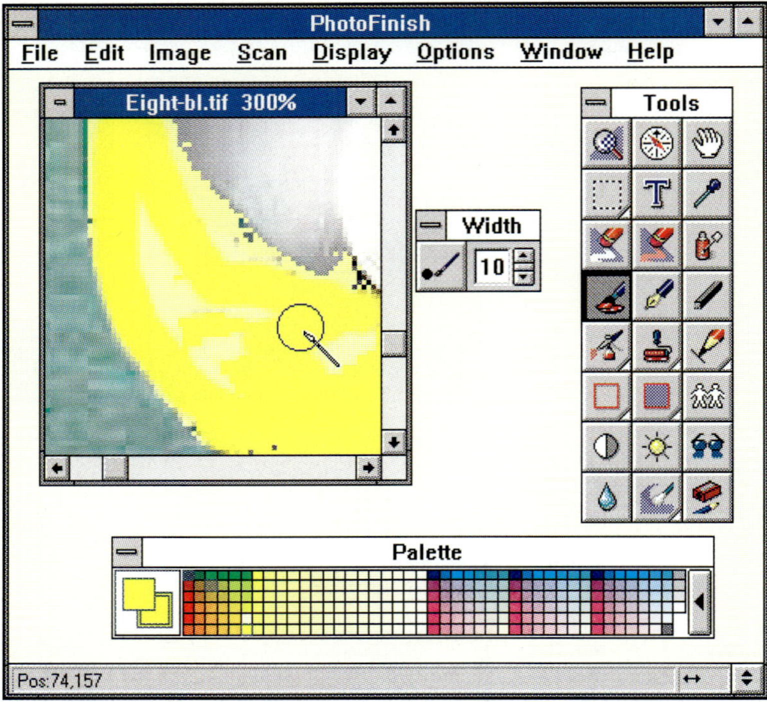

Figure C-3. We zoom in and use the Paintbrush tool to fill any gaps left by the Color Replacer.

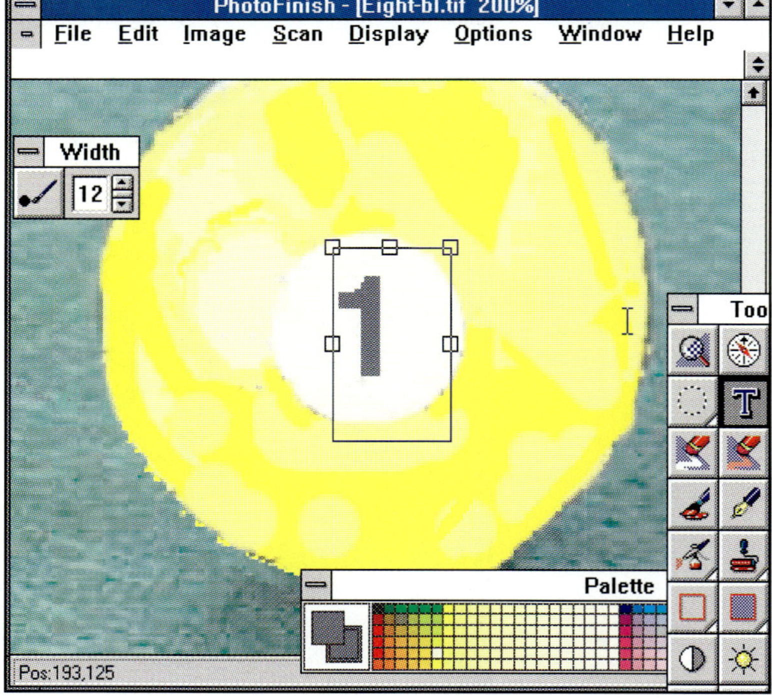

Figure C-4. Finally, we use the Text tool to add the new number.

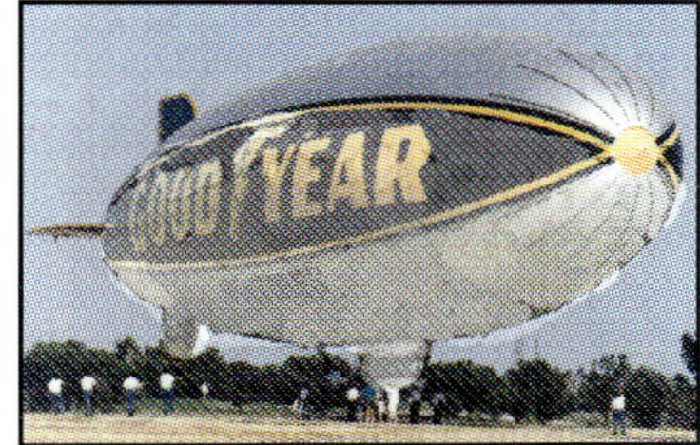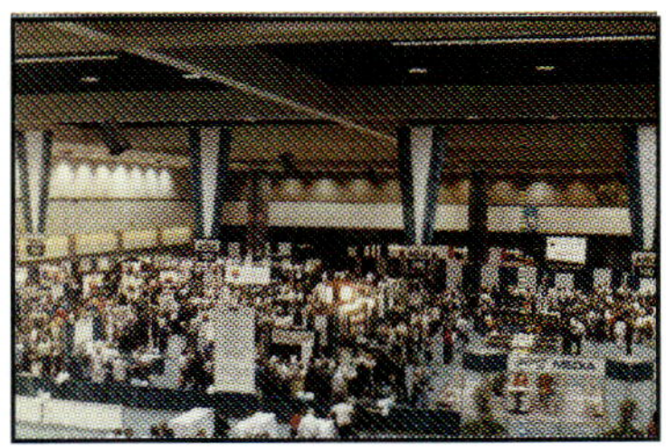

Figure C-5. We begin with two photos: the blimp and the trade show.

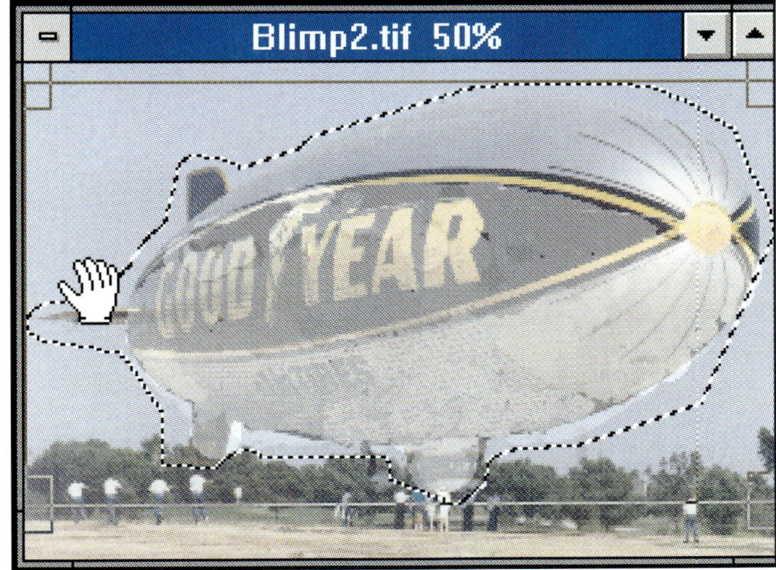

Figure C-6. After using the retouch tools to brighten the blimp, we select it using the Lasso tool.

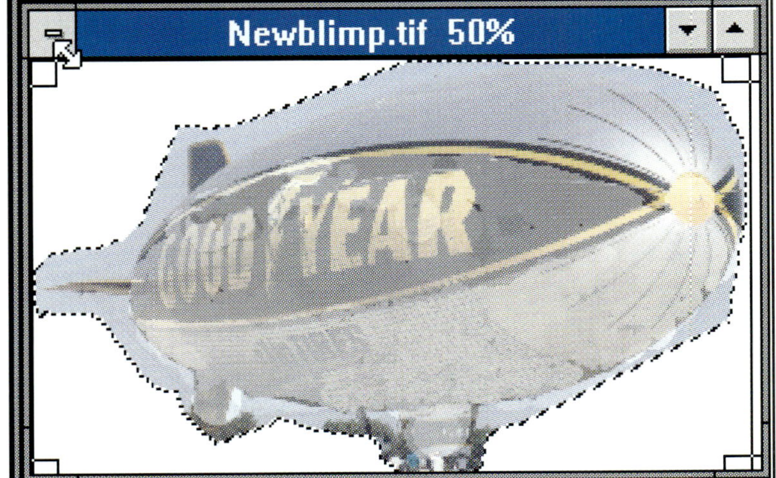

Figure C-7. We then cut-and-paste the blimp ino the new file.

• • • • • • • • • •
**Figure C-8. After
reducing the blimp, we
paste it into the trade
show shot.**

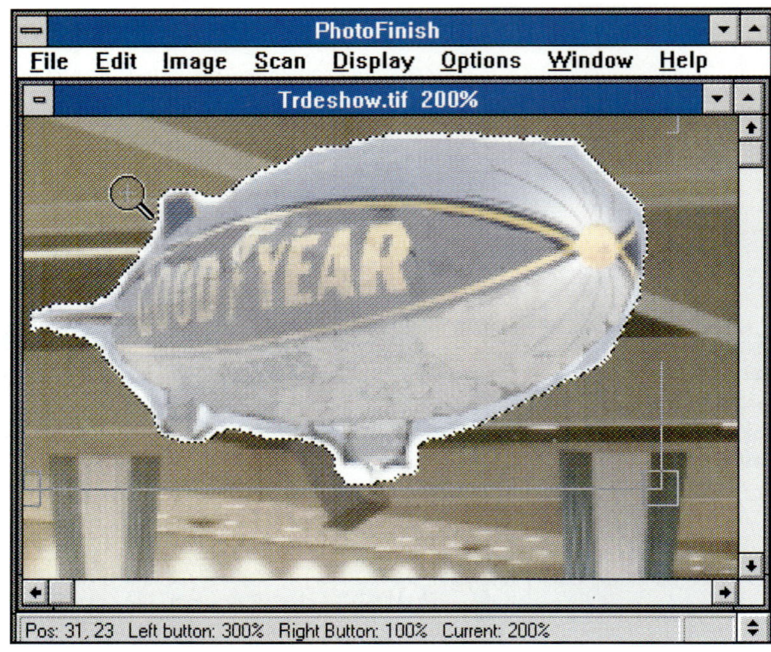

• • • • • • • • • •
**Figure C-9. We now
see the blimp flying in
the trade show.**

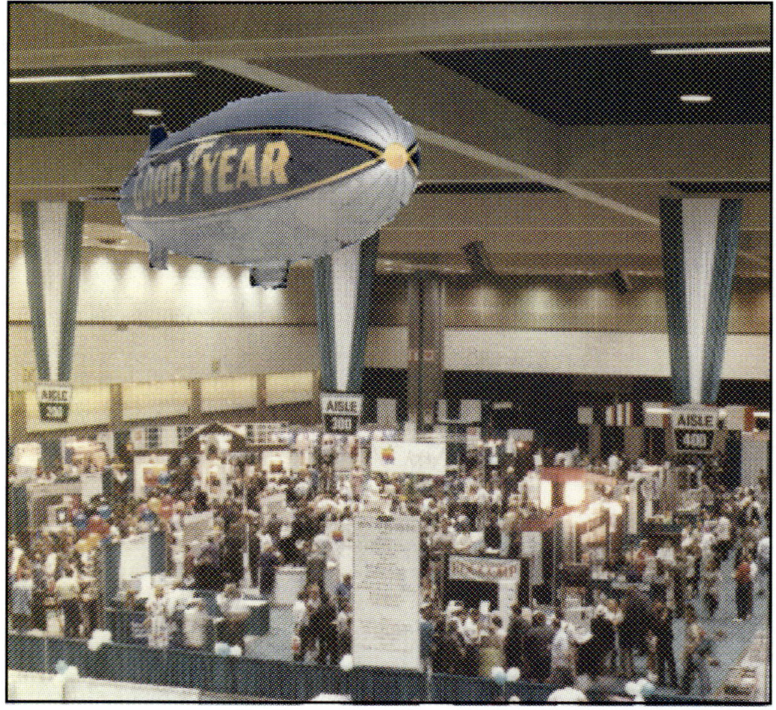

COLOR INSERT

CHAPTER 8

Working in Other Programs

In most cases, PhotoFinish is just the starting point, not the destination, for an image. The image that you scan and modify in PhotoFinish could end up in an electronic page layout, a vector-based illustration, a 35 mm slide, or a multimedia production.

In Chapter Two, we described the graphic file formats that are supported by PhotoFinish. These include TIFF, BMP, EPS, GIF, MSP, TGA, and PCX. These formats represent bridges between PhotoFinish and other software packages. When you save an image in one of these formats, it can then be imported into other programs that support those formats.

It is hard to imagine a graphics-oriented software package, especially on PC-compatible computers, that does not support one of these formats. You will even find that some of these formats, especially TIFF, are supported by programs that run on other computer systems, such as Apple's Macintosh, Commodore's Amiga, or one of the many Unix-based computers. But in case you run into the rare program that does not support TIFF, PCX, BMP, or another PhotoFinish format, you may be able to use one of the many available file conversion programs to convert the file to a format compatible with PhotoFinish.

As we noted in Chapter Two, some of the PhotoFinish image

formats are preferable to others. EPS, for example, is a format supported by many graphics programs. However, it is generally not recommended as a file transfer medium because the files tend to be very large and cannot be edited once they are saved in that format. The JPEG format, which compresses images to a fraction of their original file size, is generally not recommended because of the many different "flavors" of JPEG. If you save a file in the JPEG format, you will not necessarily be able to open it in a with other programs that support JPEG.

In this chapter, we will discuss the principal programs with which you may use PhotoFinish images. We will concentrate on page layout programs because those are probably the most popular destination for your PhotoFinish files. However, we will also discuss the use of PhotoFinish with presentation, multimedia, illustration, and other types of programs.

Page Layout Programs

Page layout programs, also known as desktop publishing programs, are software packages geared toward the production of such print materials as newspapers, magazines, newsletters, brochures, flyers, books, and catalogs. Early page layout programs were generally limited to black-and-white or spot color output and had limited graphics-handling capabilities. However, the current generation of page layout software offers powerful functions for importing, handling, and producing color images.

Page layout programs vary widely in price and capability. Some are geared primarily toward long, structured, technical documents. Others are geared toward shorter, design-intensive publications like brochures and newsletters. The most popular PC-based programs, Aldus PageMaker, Ventura Publisher, and QuarkXPress, offer features that combine these capabilities to varying degrees. Low-cost page layout programs like Microsoft Publisher and Express Publisher offer relatively limited feature sets, but also require less learning time. They are suited mostly for producing flyers and other simple one-page documents.

Some graphical word processing programs, notably Ami Professional and Microsoft Word for Windows, offer many of the same features found in page layout programs.

Aldus PageMaker

Aldus PageMaker is by most measures the most popular desktop publishing program on the market. It was one of the first software packages in this category and helped launched what has come to be known as the "desktop publishing revolution." It was also the first desktop publishing program to be available in both Macintosh and PC-compatible versions.

The PC version of PageMaker, like PhotoFinish, runs under Microsoft Windows. It supports several file formats supported by PhotoFinish, including TIFF, PCX, and BMP. The Macintosh version of PageMaker supports PC-created TIFF files without modification.

This is an important advantage, because the Macintosh TIFF format is not identical to the PC TIFF format, and some Macintosh programs cannot read PC-created TIFF files unless they are first converted to the Macintosh format. The Macintosh version of PageMaker recognizes PC TIFF files and automatically converts them to the Macintosh format.

One of PageMaker's major strengths is its highly intuitive user interface. When you launch the program, you are presented with an electronic version of a pasteup board. You can move items on or off the board as if you were working on a real-life art table. A movable toolbox on the screen provides access to tools for adding text and graphic elements. The toolbox also features a cropping tool.Graphic images (and text) are imported into PageMaker using a "Place" command. You select the command from the File menu, after which you are asked to specify the name of the file to be imported. Files can be imported either as independent or inline graphics. An independent graphic can be moved anywhere on the screen, while an inline graphic becomes part of the text. When the text moves, the graphic moves with it.

Images that are relatively small are incorporated directly into the PageMaker file. Large color images, however, are "linked." Instead of storing the image in the file, PageMaker links it to the publication. If you copy the file to a diskette for transport to a service bureau, you must also copy the graphic image or it won't be available when the service bureau opens the file.

PageMaker offers several options for manipulating graphics once they are imported. You can crop the image using the cropping tool. Simply select the tool, click in the middle of the image, and drag on the handles that appear around the image to crop on any of the four sides. One nice thing about the cropping feature is that you can easily "uncrop" the image by dragging the handles back to the original position. It's sort of like a window shade that can be opened or closed to reveal or hide the scene outside.

Images can be easily resized in PageMaker by clicking on them with the arrow tool. A set of handles appear just as they do with the cropping tool. However, instead of cropping the image, moving the handles causes the image to grow larger or smaller. You can maintain the aspect ratio—the ratio between the height and width of the image—by holding down the Shift key as you drag on the handles.

PageMaker includes an Image Control function that allows you to perform simple modifications on certain kinds of images. It is similar to the Tune Color/Gray Map function in PhotoFinish. If you have properly prepared your file in PhotoFinish, you won't need to use this function, but it's nice to know that it is there.

PageMaker, like other programs, has gone through a lengthy series of upgrades since it was first released. In early versions of PageMaker, the Image Control function worked only with gray-scale images. In addition, early versions of PageMaker for the PC could not produce color separations. If you are using one of these versions, you will probably be limited to working with gray-scale images. However, recent versions of PageMaker have sophisticated color imaging capabilities. Color separation functions are provided through a utility program known as Aldus PrePrint.

QuarkXPress

QuarkXPress has long been PageMaker's chief rival in the Macintosh environment. With its powerful functions for handling type and graphics, it has been a favorite among professional graphic designers. In 1992, Quark introduced a version of QuarkXPress that runs under Microsoft Windows. Like PageMaker, the PC version of QuarkXPress supports many file formats that are also supported by PhotoFinish, including TIFF and PCX.

QuarkXPress handles graphics a little differently from PageMaker. Instead of using a Place command to import the image and position it on the page, XPress uses what are known as "picture boxes." You click on the picture box icon on the screen, then draw the box on the page. Once you draw the box, you can then import the graphic. You can choose from several Picture Box shapes, including round, square, or polygonal, or create your own.

Cropping and scaling are also handled a little differently. When you create the picture box and import the graphic, you can place the graphic entirely within the boundaries of the box, or have it sit behind the box as if it is being viewed through a window.

If you choose the latter option, you can move the image so that different portions "peek" through the window. You can resize the image by calling up a Picture Box dialog box and entering reduction or enlargement values.

QuarkXPress offers powerful color output functions through an add-on program known as SpectreSeps QX. This program, one of many "QuarkXTensions" available for XPress, allows you to produce CYMK separations of imported TIFF files. Quark also offers an image control function, similar to the one in PageMaker, that works with color or gray-scale images. Again, it should not be necessary to use this function if you have done a good job of correcting your image in PhotoFinish.

Ventura Publisher

Ventura Publisher was one of the first popular page layout packages for PC-compatible computers. Though it is not the easiest program to learn, it can be quite productive once you master its approach to document design. It is especially strong for producing books, reports, and other long documents with a consistent format. However, it can also be used for producing newsletters, flyers, and other design-intensive publications.

The program was originally developed by a small California company called Ventura Software, which sold the marketing rights to Xerox Corp. Xerox then sold the package as "Xerox Ventura Publisher." In 1990, Xerox took over development of the program and established a subsidiary in San Diego known as Ventura Software to sell and support the package.

Ventura Publisher was one of the first page layout programs to employ what is known as a "style sheet" function. Each style sheet consists of tags that include a wide range of formatting information. For example, you can define a "bullet" tag that automatically adds a bullet to a paragraph along with any other formatting you desire. The formatting options also offer a high degree of control over character spacing, rules, and indents. This function, which makes it possible to automate many aspects of document production, has since been incorporated into competing packages like QuarkXPress and PageMaker. However, the Ventura style sheet function arguably remains the most powerful.

Ventura uses a frame-based approach to page layout. A frame is a block on the page layout that can contain text or graphics. To import a graphic, you enter Ventura's Frame mode, draw the frame on the page, then select the file to be imported. You can then crop or scale the image using commands in the Frame menu.

WORKING IN OTHER PROGRAMS

Unlike other page layout programs, Ventura Publisher does not actually incorporate image files into the publication (known as a "Chapter" in Ventura parlance). Instead, Ventura links the image in its original file to the publication. If you make changes to the original image file, they will be automatically reflected when you re-open the publication file. One consequence of this approach is that you must be sure to include the image files along with the publication (and text) files when transporting the document. Ventura includes built-in features for copying the publication and its various "constituent" files to diskettes or or other storage media for transport to a service bureau. It is important to use these built-in features when transporting files. If you simply copy the files using Windows or DOS copy commands, other users may not have access to the image files even if they are available on the disk. Ventura Publisher is available in two versions for the PC. The DOS version runs under a graphical environment known as "GEM." This was the original version of Ventura and remains popular among many users. The major advantage of the GEM version is that it runs very fast, even on relatively older, slower computers. The major disadvantage is that the GEM version has extremely limited color publishing features. You are pretty much limited to using gray-scale images.

The Windows version of Ventura Publisher, first released in 1990, includes powerful color publishing features, including the ability to produce color separations. However, the early Windows versions of Ventura suffered from many problems, including slow performance and numerous bugs. Many users who eagerly awaited the Windows edition were disappointed with the early releases, and most stuck with the GEM version. Later releases of the Windows version have corrected many of these problems. A version of Ventura Publisher is also available for the Macintosh.

FrameMaker

Frame Technology's FrameMaker is derived from a technical publishing package first offered for Unix-based workstations. It was originally developed for production of technical manuals and other long, structured documents, and these remain its forte. It includes a powerful style sheet feature similar to the one in Ventura Publisher, and also has powerful features for creating tables. It also includes powerful built-in word processing functions.

FrameMaker imports graphic images primarily in the TIFF format. Its color publishing features are weak, but it can accommodate gray-scale and spot color images.

Graphical Word Processors

Graphical word processors like Ami Professional and Microsoft Word for Windows combine word processing functions with page layout features that rival those in desktop publishing programs like PageMaker and Ventura Publisher. Both of these programs run under Microsoft Windows and are quite popular.

These programs include two modes for creating documents. In draft mode, you simply enter text as you would in a conventional word processing program. But you can also work in a layout mode that allows you to add images and other graphic elements. Working in layout mode, you can create many of the same kinds of documents you can create with a page layout program.

Ami Professional uses a page layout approach that is similar to Ventura's. It has a powerful style sheet function, and allows you to draw frames on the page in which you can import graphics. It supports several formats supported by PhotoFinish, including TIFF and PCX.

It does not include color separation functions, but is a good choice if you are satisfied with limiting yourself to gray-scale images.

Other graphical word processors include NBI's Legacy, WordStar for Windows, and Word Perfect for Windows.

Illustration Programs

In Chapter Two, we discussed the distinction between the two primary forms of computer graphics: bit-mapped and vector. While bit-mapped graphics are composed as dots, vector graphics—also known as object-oriented or draw graphics—are composed of graphic objects. On the computer screen, these objects appear as lines, curves, and shapes. Inside the computer, the graphic is stored as a series of geometric formulas.

We noted earlier that vector graphics have some advantages over bit-mapped graphics. They are resolution-independent, meaning they can be printed at the full resolution of the output device. They do a good job of reproducing text. They are also the preferred formats for storing line art, such as corporate logos or other graphic elements that must be reproduced with great precision.

Graphics packages that work with vector formats are known as "illustration" programs. Popular programs in this category include CorelDraw, Adobe Illustrator, Aldus FreeHand, and Micrografx Designer.

Instead of offering painting tools, these programs present the user with tools for creating objects. These typically include line tools, curve tools, and tools for creating geometric shapes like circles, ovals, and rectangles. One common feature in these programs is the Bezier curve tool. A Bezier curve is created by placing and manipulating points on the layout. By dragging on "control" points, you can change the shape of the curve. Most illustration programs include a freehand drawing tool that allows you to draw a curve on the screen. Once this is done, the curve is converted to a Bezier and can be reshaped by dragging on the control points.

Once you create an object, you can move it around the screen simply by clicking on it and dragging. You reshape it or resize it by dragging on handles that appear around its edges. You can define the thickness and color of the object's border. You can "fill" the object with a color, pattern, or screen.

Objects created in an illustration program can be used as elements for complex drawings. You can group multiple objects together or place them in front of or behind other objects. Some illustration programs support multiple "layers" on which you can add objects.

Many illustration program include powerful functions for manipulating text. Once you type text on the screen, you can convert it into a series of lines and curves and then manipulate it as if it were a series of objects. Some programs also include typographic features that allow you to adjust the spacing and width of characters. This makes them suitable for producing flyers, advertisements, and other documents that might otherwise be created with a page layout program.

Most of the better illustration programs have the ability to import bit-mapped images in TIFF, PCX, or other formats. This allows you to incorporate the image into an illustration as if it were a separate object. In most cases, you can crop or scale the bit-mapped image, but it cannot otherwise be modified unless you go back into PhotoFinish.

In addition to incorporating bit-mapped images into the illustration, you can also import them as "tracing templates." When you do this, a faded version of the image appears in the illustration, as if it were "underneath" a piece of tracing paper. You can then use the tools in the illustration program to trace over the bit-mapped image. Many illustration programs also include auto-trace functions that automatically convert bit-mapped images into object-oriented formats. However, they work best with simple black-and-white bit-maps.

The most popular PC-based illustration package is probably Corel Draw. More than a simple illustration drawing, Corel Draw is actually a suite of graphic tools and elements centered around a powerful drawing package. Later releases of Corel

Draw actually include a simplified version of PhotoFinish known as Photo Paint. Corel Draw also comes with an extensive library of typefaces and clip art. It supports a wide range of bit-mapped file formats—even more than PhotoFinish supports. One advantage of this is that you can use Corel Draw as a file conversion program. You can import an image in TIFF or PCX format and then export it in another format.

Other popular PC-based illustration packages include Micrografx Designer and Arts and Letters. Aldus FreeHand and Adobe Illustrator, two powerful and popular illustration packages for the Macintosh, were released in Windows versions in 1992. Both are especially popular among professional graphic designers. Micrografx, in addition to offering Designer, sells a simplified illustration program known as Windows Draw.

One category of software straddles the boundary between illustration and page layout programs. These packages include extensive text-oriented features, but also include many object-oriented graphics features. They are aimed primarily at the production of print ads, flyers, and other single-page documents. On the PC, the best known program in this category is Archetype Designer.

Presentation Programs

Presentation programs are designed for the creation of slide shows and other presentations. In some ways, they are similar to page layout programs with their ability to integrate text and graphics from a wide range of other software. However, instead of creating pages, they are used to create frames. These frames can be 35 mm slides, overhead transparencies, or screens of information presented directly from the computer. Many of these programs include powerful outlining functions that allow you to structure your presentation as you create the slides. They can also automate the production of speakers' notes.

Most presentation programs can import bit-mapped images in TIFF or other file formats. These images can then be included on slides along with text and other graphic elements. One advantage of presentation programs is that the slides they create use the RGB, instead of the CYMK, color model. We noted in Chapter Six that computer monitors do a poor job of displaying images as they will be printed because they use transmissive instead of reflective light. Slides use transmissive light, meaning that you can pretty much tell how the image will appear when you edit it on the screen in PhotoFinish.

Popular presentation programs for the PC include Aldus Persuasion, Microsoft PowerPoint, and Harvard Graphics.

Multimedia Programs

Multimedia represents one of the most exciting new developments in the computer business. The term is rather broad-ranging, but generally refers to applications that combine one or more of the following elements: text, computer graphics, animation, sound, and video.

Multimedia holds great promise as a tool for education and entertainment. One characteristic of multimedia applications is interactivity. This means that the user has control over what information is presented. A multimedia encyclopedia, for example, might offer the option of presenting video clips, sound clips, or animated diagrams of a certain topic. Multimedia also encompasses non-interactive applications, such as hardware and software systems that allow you to create your own videos.

Programs like PhotoFinish can play an important role in creation of multimedia thanks to their ability to create and manipulate photographic images. For example, you can create photorealistic scenes that can be used as backgrounds for animated characters or objects.

CHAPTER 9

Output Options

At some point after you have created or modified an image in PhotoFinish, it will probably have to be printed. It is likely that you will not actually print the image from PhotoFinish itself (though this is certainly possible). Instead, you will probably print the image from a page layout or illustration program into which you imported a PhotoFinish image.

PhotoFinish users have many alternatives when it comes to producing images. The computer market in recent years has exploded with new output options. Where you were once limited to producing output with black-and-white laser printers or low-resolution color devices, you can now turn to inkjet printers, dye-sublimation printers, imagesetters, or one of several other output technologies. In this chapter, we will look at the many output devices that can produce PhotoFinish images. We'll also say a few words about working with service bureaus.

Page Description Languages

One important element in many output devices is a page description language (PDL). A PDL is a programming language with a specialized purpose: it is designed to produce images on a laser printer, imagesetter, or other output device. The most important—and well known—PDL for computer graphics users is Adobe Systems' PostScript.

PostScript is a programming language that uses English-like commands. These commands tell an output device how to place dots on a page. You can theoretically write a PostScript program to create almost any kind of graphic object, but this is rarely practical. Instead, you rely on your graphics software—and a small program known as a PostScript "driver," to create the PostScript program. This program is then copied, or "downloaded," to the output device (Figure 9-1).

When a printer or imagesetter is said to be "PostScript-compatible," this means it can produce pages created with the PostScript PDL. Within the output device (or a related piece of hardware known as a raster-image processor or RIP) is a PostScript interpreter. The interpreter converts PostScript commands into a format that can be understood by the hardware that actually places the marks on the page.

One advantage of PostScript is device independence. This means that a page or publication produced with a program that supports PostScript can be generated with little or no modification on any PostScript printer or imagesetter. No matter what the resolution of that output device, the page can be produced at the maximum resolution and with the maximum quality.

The original version of PostScript, for all its power, had some limitations in its ability to produce high-quality color images. Some of these problems were transparent to users as hardware and software developers came up with ways to work around

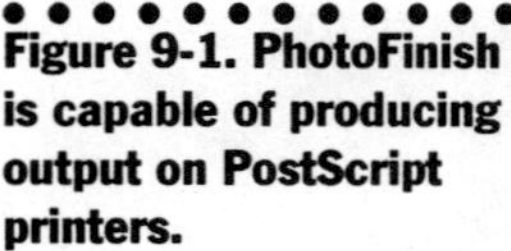

Figure 9-1. PhotoFinish is capable of producing output on PostScript printers.

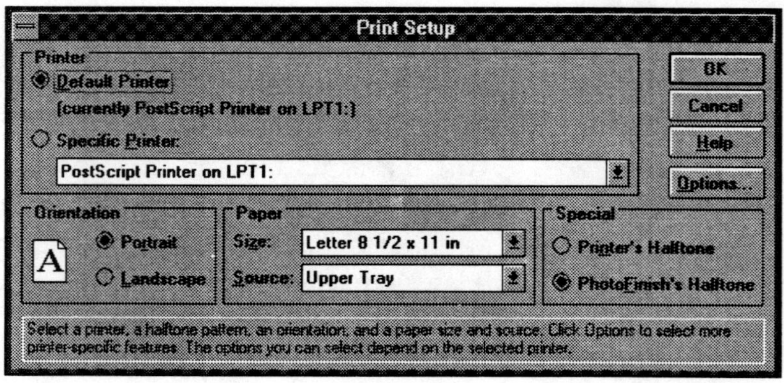

them. Adobe added many of its own "fixes"—known as extensions—that made the PDL more capable of producing color. Still, users often found that output devices were very slow when producing complex color PostScript images.

In 1990, Adobe announced PostScript Level 2, a comprehensive upgrade to the PDL. Many of the new features were aimed at color users. It supports several device-independent color spaces based on CIE 1931(XYZ)-space, a standard method for describing color that is based on human visual perception. In theory, the color space acts as a reference point to ensure consistent color output on different printers and imagesetters.

In addition to these color spaces, PostScript Level 2 includes improved algorithms for producing halftones. Some of the improvements apply to all halftones, while others are specific to color images.

 The general improvements include faster performance and the ability to specify a much wider range of halftone screen angles and frequencies.

Though PostScript is by far the most popular output standard in the desktop publishing market, some alternatives are available. In most cases, these alternatives offer a less expensive option for publishing users who balk at the relatively high cost of PostScript output devices. But as with all low-cost alternatives, there are also trade-offs in terms of quality, performance, convenience, and compatibility.

PostScript's popularity has led a number of companies to develop PostScript-compatible languages, popularly known as PostScript clones. These languages are usually packaged with interpreters and controllers that drive laser printers or imagesetters. In theory, they can interpret all PostScript commands, generating output that is identical to what a true PostScript device would produce.

PostScript clones are sold in several forms. The least expensive are software-only products that can print PostScript files on a non-PostScript printer. They tend to be very slow and usually require some form of extra memory on the computer or in the printer. Other clones are found on controllers installed in the computer or built into the printer itself. Still others are sold as cartridges that plug into the printer.

Laser Printers

Laser printers were the first computer output devices capable of producing high-quality images. Most use a technology similar to that found in office copiers. The core of the machine is a laser "engine." Within the engine, a laser heats a rotating drum or belt, producing marks where toner should go. Once the drum is heated, it fuses toner to the paper, creating recognizable images.

Another important element in the laser printer is the controller, which receives output from the computer system and converts it into instructions that drive the laser. In most PostScript printers, the controller is where the page description software resides. The controller also includes memory, which is used to store an image of the page before it is printed along with any typefaces resident in the printer or downloaded from the computer. In some cases, the controller can also be connected to a hard disk, which is used to store extra typefaces.

In addition to being black-and-white devices, most early laser printers were limited to 300-dpi resolution. This resolution is suitable for producing line art, but is woefully inadequate for producing high-quality halftones.

However, some newer models offer much higher resolutions, along with controller technology designed to produce the best-looking halftones possible with the technology. Halftones produced by these printers are suitable for use in newspapers and other publications with relatively modest quality requirements.

Color Printers

Printers capable of color output use a wide variery of technologies. They range from relatively inexpensive inkjet models to dye-transfer printers capable of producing output that is nearly indistinguishable from photographs. These printers cannot produce color separations, but they provide a quick way for publishers to generate proofs of pages that will eventually be produced on a PostScript imagesetter or color separation system. In addition to inkjet and dye-transfer technologies, some color printers use what's known as thermal wax-transfer technology (Figure 9-2).

Thermal-Transfer Printers

In a thermal-transfer engine, a print head melts tiny dots of plastic or wax into the paper (Figure 9-3). The plastic or wax is stored on sheets or ribbons, contained in a cartridge, that scroll through the printer in much the same way that film moves through a camera. Most cartridges come in one of two varieties: three-color and four-color. The three-color cartridges use cyan, yellow, and magenta as their primary colors, while the four-color versions add black. Cyan, yellow, and magenta can be combined to create black, but the printers generally get better results using all four primary colors, especially when producing text output in black ink.

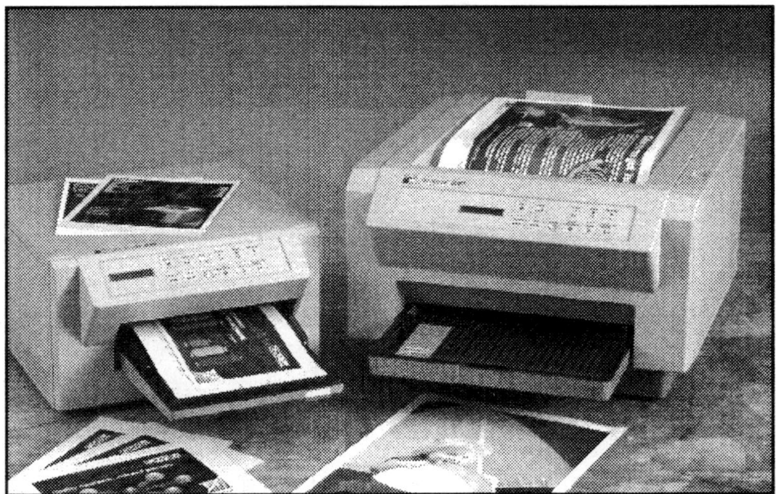

Figure 9-2. Thermal-transfer printers are a popular means of producing color output.

Thermal wax-transfer printers can do an adequate job of producing color pages, but they have some limitations. Photographic images tend to have a grainy, dithered appearance that results from the way dots are laid on the page. As a result, these printers do a poor job of predicting how a color print job will look on press. In addition, they are limited in the kinds of media they can handle. They generally require thermal paper or transparency film for best printing results.

Inkjet Printers

In an inkjet printer, ink in three or four of the primary color is sprayed through tiny nozzles on to the page. Beyond this, color inkjet printers vary widely in price and capability.

At the low end, several manufacturers offer 300-dpi color inkjet printers for less than $1000. Output quality is close to, but not quite as good as, that of thermal wax-transfer printers. But these printers are also very slow.

Some color printers, notably models from Dataproducts and Tektronix, use solid ink technology. The major advantage of solid-ink technology is that it can print on nearly any kind of paper stock.

This is especially important when the printer is used as a

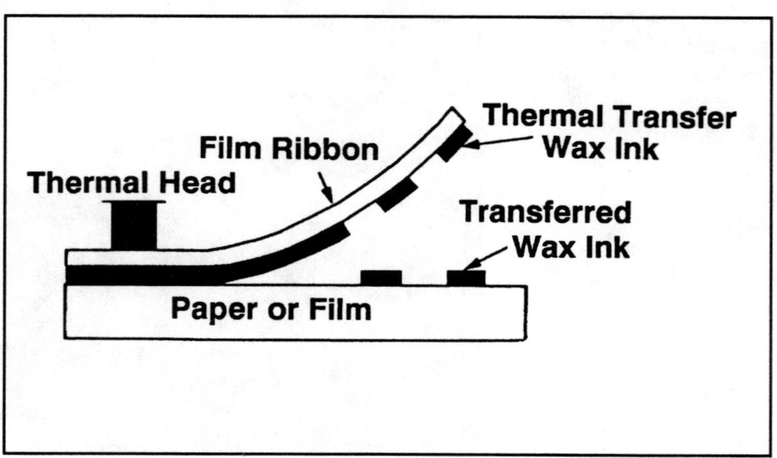

Figure 9-3. A thermal-transfer engine melts tiny dots of plastic or wax into the paper.

proofing device, because the user can print on paper that more closely approximates the stock used to reproduce the output.

Solid ink is installed in the form of "color sticks" for each of the four primary colors: cyan, yellow, magenta, and black. The ink melts almost instantly at a certain temperature, but solidifies just as quickly slightly below that temperature. When sprayed on the page, the ink dries before it can be absorbed, most of it remaining on the surface of the paper.

One limitation of solid-ink technology is that it does not do a good job of printing on transparencies. Solid inks tend to have a "beaded" texture that distorts light passing through the medium.

At the high end, a company called Iris Graphics offers a series of inkjet printers that can produce photorealistic images on nearly any kind of paper stock (Figure 9-4).

These images are also known as continuous-tone images because each dot can be a varying shade of color. These

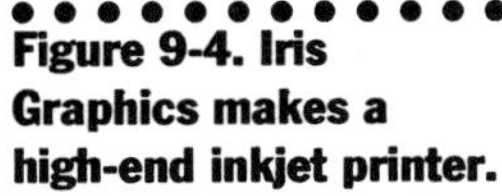

Figure 9-4. Iris Graphics makes a high-end inkjet printer.

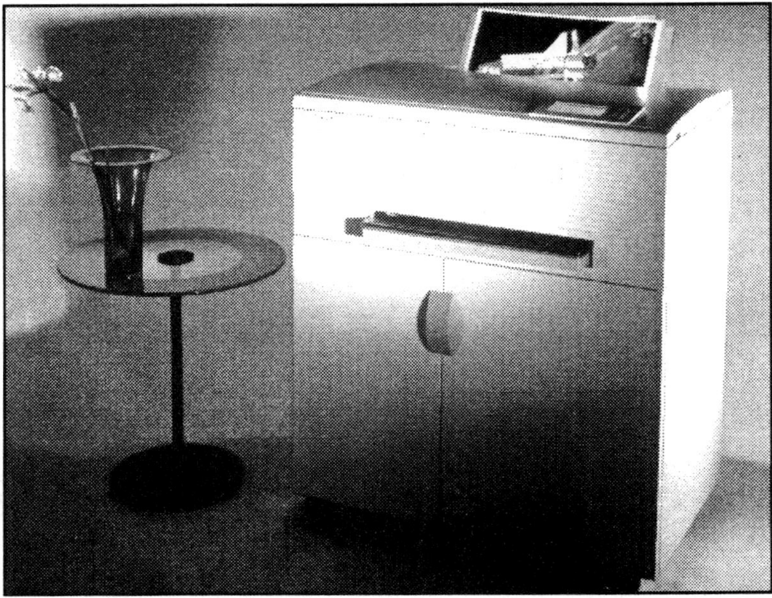

printers produce output of outstanding quality, but they are also quite expensive at $30,000 or more.

Dye Transfer Printers

Dye transfer, also known as dye-sublimation technology, is a variation on thermal-transfer technology (Figure 9-5). A thermal print head transfers dye from a ribbon to the paper or film on which the image is to be printed.

Unlike conventional thermal-transfer printers, which melt tiny dots of wax or plastic onto the page, dye-sublimation printers can vary the intensity of each dot. This makes it possible to produce continuous-tone images. However, the technology is limited to printing on transparency film or a special kind of thermal paper.

Dye transfer printers used to be very expensive, but have come down considerably in price. They are a favorite of photographers and fine artists because their output looks almost indistinguishable from a quality color photograph.

However, they have limited usefulness as proofing devices because they don't necessarily foretell how a page will look when printed on an offset press.

Figure 9-5. Dye transfer printers are capable of producing photographic output.

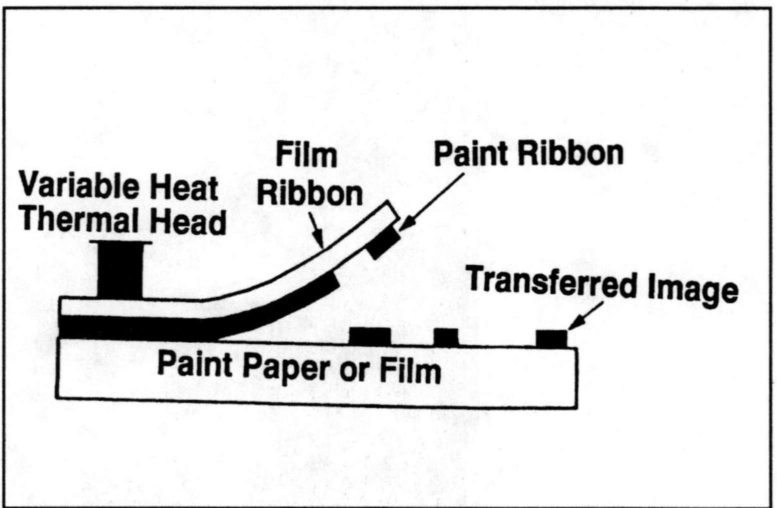

Color Copiers

Another important printing trend in recent years is the digital color copier. These products, which include Canon's CLC 500 and Kodak's ColorEdge, can produce color copies just like a standard photocopier produces black-and-white prints. However, they also feature digital interfaces, which means they can be connected to a computer system.

Several companies offer interface products that permit computer output on a digital color copier. In addition to the actual interface, these products include PostScript (or PostScript clone) interpreters, extra memory, and software that automatically color-corrects images to produce high-quality output. The best of these products allow the color copier to produce continuous-tone images similar to what a dye-sublimation printer can produce.

The most popular of these products is the Fiery controller from Electronics for Imaging (EFI). Prints produced from a Fiery-equipped copier are often known as "Fiery" prints (Figure 9-6).

Color copiers—and interface products like the Fiery—are very

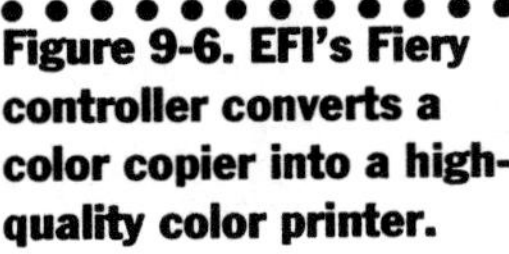

Figure 9-6. EFI's Fiery controller converts a color copier into a high-quality color printer.

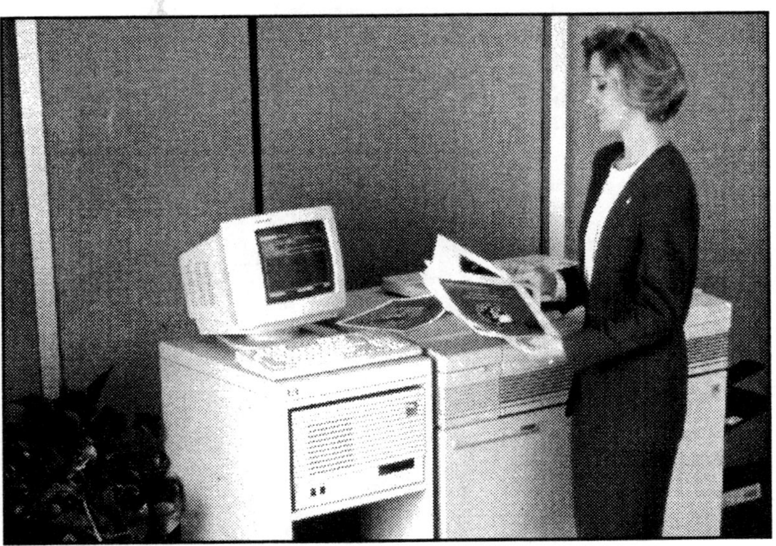

expensive. However, many service bureaus are now offering output on Canon CLC 500 copiers with the Fiery controller.

Color Plotters

Another recent trend in the computer graphics market is large-format color output. Many service bureaus have installed electrostatic or inkjet plotters that can produce PostScript files at sizes ranging up to 52 inches by 30 feet. Output resolution ranges from 200 to 400 dpi.

Large-format output systems are used in a wide range of applications. One of the most popular is trade show signage. Other popular applications include retail point-of-sale displays, shopping mall signage, courtroom displays, and business presentations.

Most large-format output systems are based on an electrostatic plotter from Xerox Corp. known as the Versatec. This plotter

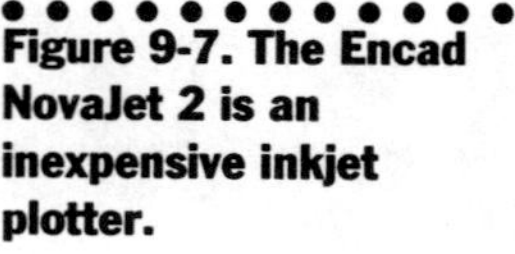

Figure 9-7. The Encad NovaJet 2 is an inexpensive inkjet plotter.

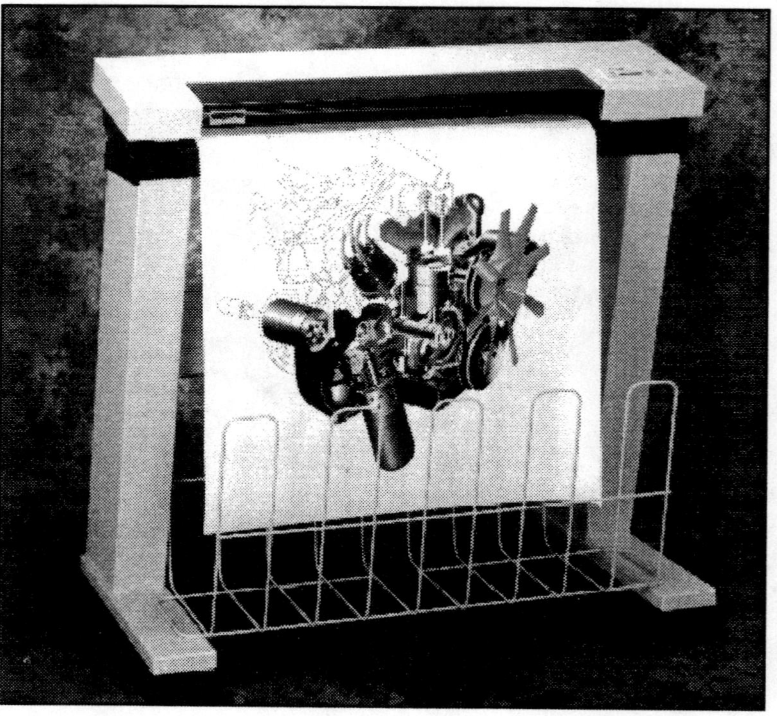

is available in two models, one capable of output up to 42 inches wide, the other capable of 52-inch output. It uses roll-fed paper, meaning the length of the output is nearly unlimited.

By itself, the Versatec plotter cannot produce PostScript output. However, several companies have developed hardware products that produce PostScript output on electrostatic plotters from Xerox and other companies. Some of these products are geared toward producing large-format photographic output. You can submit a photographic image on a disk and have it produced at sizes big enough to cover most of a wall.

One popular large-format output product is known as MegaChrome. MegaChrome is actually a trade name for several systems offered by ReproCAD, a national network of architectural reprographics firms. ReproCAD-member companies are found in most major cities. They are the only companies that can offer the MegaChrome service. Though these companies originated in the architectural business, they can produce output for a wide range of customers. MegaChrome, like many other large-format systems, uses a PostScript clone interpreter based on Freedom of Press software from CAI.

Several other companies offer systems that allow PostScript output on the Versatec plotter. A Palo Alto, CA, company called Colossal Graphics offers the PowerScript system. A New Jersey company called Cactus offers a version of the Versatec plotter with an Adobe-licensed PostScript processor. Visual Edge Technology in south San Francisco offers a system aimed primarily at photographic output.

Synergy Computer Graphics of Sunnyvale, CA offers a large-format PostScript system based on its own 36-inch plotter. The Synergy plotter uses an Adobe-licensed PostScript RIP. CalComp, one of the leading manufacturers in the CAD market, introduced its 68000 electrostatic plotter in 1992. The plotter works with several PostScript-compatible front-ends.

Electrostatic plotters are expensive, so most users will produce large-format output by going to a service bureau. Prices vary widely, but are generally charged by the square foot.

A San Diego, CA company called Encad offers an inexpensive color plotter called the NovaJet 2 (Figure 9-7) that offers 300-dpi output up to 36 inches in width. The plotter, which carries a $10,000 price tag, does not include PostScript capability. However, Colossal Graphics has developed a PostScript-compatible front end for the system that costs about $15,000, including the plotter. One disadvantage of the NovaJet is that it is much slower than electrostatic plotters.

High-Resolution Imagesetters

So far, we have discussed output devices that produce composite color prints—that is, full-color prints. These prints may be nice to look at, but they are not suitable for reproduction on press. If you want to reproduce more than a few copies of your PhotoFinish images, you need to turn to an output device capable of producing color separations. In most cases, this means turning to a service bureau equipped with a high-resolution PostScript imagesetter.

Imagesetters capable of producing high-resolution mono-chrome and color separation output are descended from the phototypesetters first developed in the 1950s. Like these early ancestors, imagesetters produce output on photographic film or resin-coated paper. However, they are capable of producing complete page layouts, including images, unlike traditional phototypesetters that could only produce type galleys.

The history of the PostScript imagesetter begins in 1986, with Linotype's introduction of the Linotronic 100 and 300 along with the RIP 1. Three years earlier, Linotype had signed an agreement with Adobe Systems giving the PostScript developer rights to use typefaces from the German manufacturer's extensive type library. As part of the deal, Linotype won the right to incorporate the PostScript language into its laser-driven phototypesetters.

These products were relatively primitive by current standards, but the basic technology remains the same. A PostScript file is produced with a desktop publishing or graphics package and downloaded from a personal computer to the raster image processor (RIP). Here, the PostScript language commands are converted into an electronic array of tiny dots. This information is passed to the image recorder, where a laser beam exposes the dots onto photosensitive film or paper. The photosensitive medium is then removed from the recorder and sent through a chemical processor, which produces the final output in much the same way a photo processing lab develops your snapshots.

The major limitation in these early imagesetters was the RIP. With its limited memory and speed, Linotype's original RIP 1 had difficulty handling complex pages, especially those that included halftones or other images. Subsequent RIPs have steadily improved in performance and imaging capabilities. Today's imagesetters are capable of producing color separations at 3000 dots per inch or more in addition to standard monochrome output.

Leading manufacturers of PostScript imagesetters include Linotype-Hell, Agfa, Scitex, Optronics, Varityper, and Birmy Graphics. Linotype-Hell and Agfa are the two market leaders.

Early imagesetters, such as the Linotronic 300 and Agfa 9400, were suitable mainly for producing type, line art, and black-and-white halftones. Though some hardy pioneers experimented with producing color separations on these machines, output quality was suspect. Early RIPs were also very slow when handling complex images, even in monochrome.

Another limitation in early imagesetters was dot repeatability. To produce process color on a printing press, the user must provide separations corresponding to the four primary colors, cyan, yellow, magenta, and black (CYMK). When these primaries are combined in various percentages, they can produce a wide variety of acceptable colors. On the press each full-color image receives four impressions of ink once for each separation.

For this to work, however, each dot on each of the four separations must be positioned with a high degree of precision. Otherwise, the output will suffer from misregistration and moire patterns.

Early imagesetters designed primarily for monochrome output often were not up to this task. Though they were adequate for simple spot color jobs, they did not offer the kind of precise dot repeatability needed for quality process color work.

One culprit was the feeding mechanism used to pull the paper or film media through the image recorder. Most early imagesetters use a roller feed (also known as "capstan") mechanism that lacked the ability to precisely align dots from one separation to another.

In the years since, imagesetter manufacturers have developed capstan mechanisms that offer much improved repeatability. In addition, several companies have introduced imagesetters that use drum-based mechanisms similar to those found in high-end color pre-press systems.

One pioneer in this area was Optronics, whose ColorSetter uses a rotating drum with registration pins similar to the tractor feed sprockets on a dot matrix printer along with a vacuum mechanism to hold the film in place.

Optronics claims that this drum mechanism offers overall repeatability of 5 microns about one-fifteenth the diameter of a human hair.

Other manufacturers of drum-based imagesetters include Scitex, Linotype-Hell, and Agfa. In addition to offering a more precise feeding mechanism, some of these imagesetters provide a relatively large imaging area that allows production of signatures for use on a web press.

Prepress Links

Leading developers of high-end color prepress systems, including Crosfield, Scitex, Linotype-Hell, and Dainippon Screen, have introduced products that provide links to PostScript-based desktop publishing systems.

These links tend to be quite expensive, but they also offer the best of two worlds: the high-quality image output of a proprietary prepress system along with the convenience and control of desktop publishing. These links are most often found in traditional color separation houses, which can take advantage of the desktop publishing revolution while justifying their large investment in high-end prepress systems that can cost as much as $1 million.

In a typical scenario, the user submits a desktop publishing file along with color transparencies. The system operator scans the transparencies with a drum scanner and incorporates the images into the page layout. The operator then produces the color separations with images and text in place.

Proofing Systems

Most service bureaus that have made a heavy commitment to color output offer film-based proofing systems from Du Pont, 3M, Enco, and other manufacturers. Color publishing experts will tell you that these film-based proofs are the only practical option if you want an accurate idea of how a page will appear in print.

Working With Service Bureaus

You can see that the service bureau is likely to play an important role in your efforts to produce color images from PhotoFinish. Therefore, a few words about working with service bureaus are in order.

Many users of Microsoft Windows products have found that service bureaus are lacking when it comes to producing PC output. Most service bureaus are primarily oriented toward Apple's Macintosh. They may know Macintosh applications inside and out, and may be proficient at spotting problems in Macintosh files that will lead to output difficulties. But when it comes to Windows output, they are woefully inadequate.

One problem is Windows itself. Service bureau managers often complain that Windows presents problems that they don't have to deal with in the Macintosh world. Because Windows handles all printing from the Windows environment, this can be a serious problem. However, many service bureaus have managed to work around the problems presented by Windows and can do an adequate, or even excellent job, of producing Windows output. As Windows-based graphics applications grow more popular, more service bureaus will no doubt jump on the bandwagon.

If you want to avoid Windows-related service bureau problems, your best solution is to find a service bureau that understands Windows. It will also help if you are using an application, such as PageMaker or Corel Draw, that service bureaus are familiar with.

When looking for a service bureau, ask the following questions:

What percentage of your color output is from Windows, as opposed to the Macintosh?

Do you produce Windows output directly from Windows, or do you simply copy PostScript files to the Macintosh and produce them from the Mac?

Do you accept PostScript files only, or can you also produce output directly from the application?

What Windows applications do you have in-house? Which ones are you familiar with?

Don't be afraid to ask for references. Be sure to ask about other Windows users, preferably those who are doing jobs similar to yours.

Keep in mind that the service bureau business is highly competitive, and they want your business. On the downside, this means service bureau reps may be inclined to overstate their ability to produce Windows output. On the other hand, if they want to keep your business, they should know that they have to do a good job of serving you. Otherwise, you can always go to the service bureau across town.

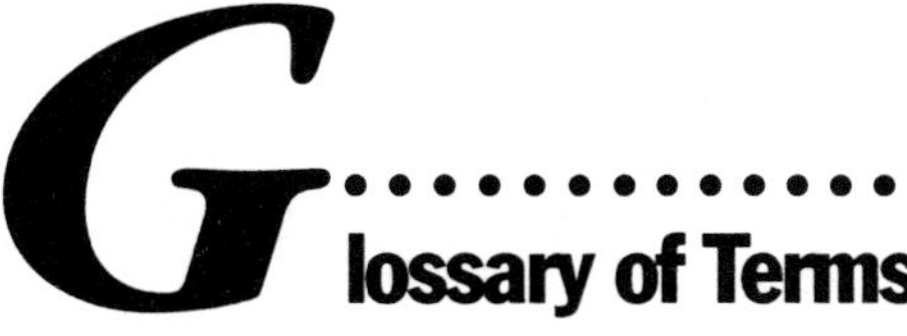

Glossary of Terms

Architecture. The specific components, and the way those components are interconnected, that make up a microcomputer system. Often used to describe the specific bus structure within a microcomputer.

ASCII. American Standard Code for Information Interchange. A standard coding system that assigns a numeric value to letters, numbers and symbols. The lowest common denominator for exchanging text among programs.

Aspect Ratio. The relationship between the height and width of a displayed object. A 1:1 aspect ratio means the object will appear undistorted.

Auto Trace. A feature found in some graphics programs that allows conversion of bit-mapped images into an object-oriented format. See Bit-map, Object-oriented graphics.

Bernoulli. A removable hard disk system popular in the PC-compatible. Bernoulli disks can hold 44 or 90 megabytes of data and are manufactured by Iomega Corp.

Bezier curves. A type of curve created by some object-oriented graphics programs that can be manipulated by means of endpoints and anchor points that determine its slope and length.

Binary. A numbering system employed by most computer systems that uses two numerals, 0 and 1, to represent all numbers.

Bit. The smallest unit of binary information. A bit will have a value of "1" or "0". A contracted acronym derived from Binary digIT.

Bit-Map. Images formed by patterns of dots, as opposed to object-oriented images, where shapes are formed from mathematical descriptions.

Bit-Mapped Display. A computer display that can control individual pixels, allowing the computer to show graphics in addition to text. See Character-Based Display.

Brightness. A measure of lightness or darkness in an image.

Bus. A data pathway within a computer system.

Byte. A unit of data containing eight bits. A byte can consist of up to 256 different values. Used as a measure of file size on a computer. See Kilobyte, Megabyte.

Calibration. A process by which a scanner, monitor, or output device is adjusted to provide more accurate display and reproduction of images.

Camera-Ready Copy. Text and illustrations laid out on a page in the proper size and position, and ready to be photographed for a printing plate. See Mechanicals.

Cathode-Ray Tube. (CRT). A vacuum tube that generates and guides electrons onto a fluorescent screen to produce images, characters, or graphics.

CCD. See Charge-Coupled Device.

CD-ROM. (Compact-Disc Read-Only Memory) An optical disc capable of storing computer data. Often used for distribution of clip art, fonts, and multimedia titles. Data can be read from a CD-ROM, but cannot be written to the disc.

Central Processing Unit (CPU). The main section of a computer, which handles arithmetic and logic operations.

CGA. Short for Color Graphics Adapter, the first color display standard for PC-compatible computers. Offers limited resolution. See EGA, Hercules, VGA.

CGM. see Computer Graphics Metafile.

Character-Based Display. A computer display, commonly found in the first personal computers, that is limited to showing alphanumeric characters and simple graphic elements. Most character-based displays use a grid consisting of 25 rows and 80 columns. Each cell in the grid can contain only a single character.

Charge-Coupled Device (CCD). An image sensor used in scanners and digital cameras.

Clipboard. A temporary electronic storage area in a computer system where text or graphics can be held for reuse.

Color Correction. A process of adjusting color values to achieve the best level of accuracy for a reproduction.

Color Separation. A process by which a color page is converted into CYMK color components. Each color can be used to create a piece of film, which is burned onto a plate or written directly to a printing press. See CYMK.

Color Separations. A set of four transparencies for making plates in four-color printing.

Comp. See Comprehensive.

Comprehensive. A page, produced during the design process, that provides a preview of how the final print job will look.

Computer Graphics Metafile (CGM). A file format used for storing computer graphics.

Continuous Tone. A photograph or illustration containing an infinite range of colors or gray shades.

Contrast. A measure of the difference among various colors or gray levels in an image. A high-contrast image shows a large difference between light and dark shades. A low-contrast image shows less difference between light and dark shades.

CPU. See Central Processing Unit.

Crop Marks. Small marks on a page that indicate the area to be printed.

Crop. To cut or trim an illustration or other graphic element.

CRT. See Cathode-Ray Tube.

CYMK. Cyan, Yellow, Magenta, Black. These four colors are used by printers to reproduce color images.

Data Compression. An operation that reduces the memory space required to store image data.

Default. A specification that takes effect in the absence of other instructions. Most scanner programs have default settings for variables like brightness and contrast that apply unless the user requests something else.

Densitometer. A device used to measure the intensity of gray shades or colors in a printed image. Often used to calibrate an imagesetter, scanner, or monitor for more accurate display and reproduction of images.

Desktop Publishing. The use of a personal computer to produce camera-ready page layouts for books, newsletters, magazines, and other printed material. Also refers to programs that produce page layouts. See Page-Layout Program.

Dialog Box. A pop-up window in a program that allows the user to choose among different options.

Diffusion. A filtering effect performed on gray-scale or color images that randomly distributes gray levels in small areas of an image to achieve a mezzotint effect.

Digital Halftone. A halftone produced by a computer system. See Halftone.

Digitize. To convert information to the digital format usable by a computer. What scanners and digitizers do.

Digitizer. A device that converts video signals into a digital format that can be displayed on a computer. Also used to refer to certain computer drawing devices.

Disk Operating System (DOS). An operating system for IBM-compatible personal computers that controls basic computer operations, such as the transfer of data to and from a disk drive. Requires use of English-like commands to perform operations. Also known as MS-DOS and PC-DOS.

Dithering. A process by which an input or output device simulates shades of gray in an image by grouping dots into clusters known as halftone cells. See Halftone cell.

DOS. See Disk Operating System.

Dot. The smallest unit that can be printed, scanned, or displayed on a monitor. Dots produced on a laser printer are sometimes called spots.

Dots Per Inch (DPI). A unit that describes the resolution of an output device or monitor.

DPI. See Dots Per Inch.

Driver. A software program that controls a specific hardware device such as a frame grabber board, scanner, or printer.

Drum Imagesetter. An imagesetter in which the output media is mounted on a rotating drum.

Drum Scanner. A scanner in which reflective or transmissive media are mounted on a rotating drum.

Dye Sublimation. A color printing technology used in continuous-tone printers.

Edge Enhancement. An operation that accentuates the edge details of an image.

EGA. Short for Enhanced Graphics Adapter, a color display standard in the PC-compatible environment. Offers better resolution and color display than CGA, but is surpassed by VGA. See CGA, Hercules, VGA.

Encapsulated PostScript (EPS). A file format that stores images in the form of PostScript language commands.

EPS. See Encapsulated PostScript File.

Equalization. A process by which the range of gray or color shades in an image is expanded to make the image more attractive.

Facsimile. A technology that allows transmission of images over telephone lines by use of facsimile machines or PC fax boards.

Filter. A software function that modifies an image by altering the gray or color values of certain pixels.

Flatbed scanner. A scanner, resembling a small photocopier, in which the image to be scanned is placed on a glass platen.

Font. All letters, numbers, and symbols in one size and typeface. Helvetica Bold Italic is a typeface. 12-point Helvetica bold italic is a font. Font is sometimes used interchangeably with typeface.

Four-color printing. A process that allows a printing press to reproduce most colors by mixing the three primary colors (cyan, yellow, magenta) and black.

Frame Buffer. Memory used to store an array of graphic or pictorial image data. Each element of the array corresponds to one or more pixels in a video display or one or more dots on a laser printer or other output device.

Frame-Grabber Board. An image processing board that samples, digitizes, stores and processes video signals. Typically, a frame grabber board will plug into one expansion slot within a microcomputer.

Frame. A block positioned on a page into which the user can place text or graphics.

Galley. In typesetting terminology, a reproduction of a column of type, usually printed on a long paper sheet.

Gamma Correction. A process by which the user adjusts the midtone contrast and brightness of an image.

Gamma Curve Editor. A function found in many imaging programs that allows the user to perform gamma correction operations on a color or gray-scale image. Also known as a Gray or Color Map Editor.

Graphical User Interface (GUI). A computer interface, such as Microsoft Windows, characterized by the use of a bit-mapped display and graphical icons that represent common computer functions.

Gray Scale Value. A number with a range between 0 and 255 that represents the brightness level of an individual pixel in a gray scale image document.

Gray Scale. A measure of the number of gray levels in an image. Also used to describe the ability to display multiple levels of gray.

GUI. See Graphical User Interface.

Hand Scanner. A small scanner that requires the user to manually move the unit over the image to be scanned.

Halftone cell. A halftone dot created on a laser printer or imagesetter. The cell is created by grouping printer dots into a grid. The more dots present in the grid, the larger the cell appears.

Halftone. A type of photograph that can be reproduced by a printing press. A halftone breaks a continuous-tone photo into tiny dots, which the press can reconstruct with ink. The eye interprets the dots as tones and shades. The density of the dot pattern, called a screen, determines the ultimate quality of the printed reproduction. A halftone can be a positive or a negative. See Screen.

Hardware. Mechanical, magnetic, electronic, and electrical devices that make up computer. Physical equipment that makes up a computer system.

Hercules. A monochrome graphics display standard used in the PC-compatible environment. See CGA, EGA, VGA.

Histogram. A graph showing the distribution of gray or color levels within an image. The horizontal coordinate is the pixel value. The vertical coordinate shows the number of pixels in the image that use the value. Histograms give a good indication of image contrast and brightness dynamic range.

Horizontal Resolution. The number of pixels contained in a single horizontal scanning line.

Illustration Program. A program used to create object-oriented graphics. See Object-Oriented Graphics.

Imagesetter. A high-resolution output device, descended from the phototypesetter, that produces output on film or photographic paper at resolutions of 1000 dots per inch or more. Usually employs a page description language like PostScript.

Inkjet Printer. A nonimpact printer that uses droplets of ink. As a printhead moves across surface of paper, it shoots a stream of tiny, electrostatically-charged ink drops at the page, placing them to form characters.

Interpolation. A mathematical technique used in some scanning and graphics programs that can be used to increase the apparent resolution of an image. Computers usually store images as numbers that represent the intensity of the image at discrete points. Interpolation generates values for points in between these discrete points by looking at the surrounding intensities.

Joint Photographic Experts Group (JPEG). An international standard for compression and decompression of photographic images.

JPEG. See Joint Photographic Experts Group.

Kilobyte. A measurement unit used to describe the size of computer files. A kilobyte is equivalent to 1024 bytes or characters of information.

Landscape. Horizontal orientation of pages or screen displays. See Portrait.

Laser Printer. A non-impact output device that fuses toner to paper to create near-typeset quality text and graphics. The basic technology is similar to that of a photocopier.

Layout. The arrangement of a page, especially the spacing and position of text and graphics. Often used to describe a rough sketch.

LCD. See Liquid-Crystal Display.

LED. See Light-Emitting Diode.

Light-Emitting Diode (LED). A form of display lighting employed on many different office, reprographic, and consumer products.

Line Art. A drawing that contains no grays or middle tones. Even when cross-hatching and other techniques are used to simulate shading, line art is made up exclusively of black (lines) and white (paper).

Line Screen. A measure of the screen frequency, or resolution, of a halftone. Most printed halftones have line screens ranging from 65 lines per inch to 150 lines per inch.

Linotronic. The brand name for imagesetters manufactured by Linotype-Hell, including the Linotronic 330 and Linotronic 630.

Liquid-Crystal Display (LCD). LCD screens are made up of liquid crystals sandwiched between two glass plates. They are typically small and flat, and require very little power for operation.

Lithography. See Offset printing.

Local-Area Network. A system that connects microcomputers to one another, allowing them to share data and output devices.

Lossless. An image-compression function in which image data is not lost every time the compression is performed.

Lossy. An image-compression function in which image data is lost every time the compression is performed.

LPI. Abbreviation for lines per inch. Used to measure halftone resolution.

Mechanicals. Camera-ready pages on artboards or flats, with text and art in position. See Camera-ready copy.

Megabyte. A measurement unit used to describe the size of computer files. A megabyte is equivalent to 1024 kilobytes, or 1,048,576 characters of information.

Microprocessor. A single chip or integrated circuit containing an entire central processing unit for a personal computer or computer-based device.

Microsoft Windows. A software application developed by Microsoft that manages data displayed on the CRT screen in rectangular areas known as windows. The user interacts with the software by selecting icons and menu items from the screen.

Modem. A device that allows computers to send and receive information over phone lines.

Moire Pattern. An undesirable grid-like pattern in a digital halftone resulting from the superimposition of dot-screens at wrong screen angles. Usually occurs when a halftone has been rescanned or if a dithered image has been scaled.

Mouse. A small, hand-held device for positioning the cursor on the screen. When the mouse is rolled across the surface of the desk, the cursor moves a corresponding distance on the screen.

MS-DOS. A disk operating system used widely with personal computers and developed by Microsoft Corp.

MSP. The graphics format used by Microsoft Windows Paint.

Multimedia. A category of computer applications character- ized by the combination of sound, video, and/or animation.

Object-Oriented Graphics. Graphic images created by means of mathematical descriptions. They can usually be displayed or printed at the full resolution of the monitor or output device, offering more precision than bit-mapped images.

OCR. See Optical Character Recognition.

Offset Printing. A widely used printing process in which a page is reproduced photographically on a metal plate attached to a revolving cylinder. Ink is transferred from the plate to a rubber blanket from which it is transferred to paper.

Operating System. Master programs that keep all of computer components working together, including application programs.

Optical Disk. A form of data storage in which a laser records data on a disk that can be read with a lower-power laser pickup. There are three types of optical disks: Read Only (RO), Write-Once Read Many (WORM), and two types of erasable: Thermo Magneto Optical (TMO) and Phase Change (PC).

Overlay. A sheet laid on top of a page for spot-color printing.

Page Description Language. A programming language, such as PostScript, that gives precise instructions for how a page should look to an output device. See PostScript.

Page-Layout Program. A computer program that allows the user to create page layouts for newsletters, newspapers, magazines, and other printed materials. Also known as desktop publishing or page layout programs.

Paint Program. A program used to create bit-mapped graphics. See Bit-map.

Palette. The set of all colors available for screen displays.

Panning. Moving a graphic image inside a frame to see its various sections.

Pantone Matching System. A popular system for specifying spot colors. Each color has its own Pantone number by which it can be selected. See Spot color.

PC-compatible. A computer system compatible with the IBM-PC and its descendants.

PCX. A graphic file format developed by ZSoft. Supported by many scanners and publishing programs.

Photo CD. A technology developed by Eastman Kodak that allows storage of photographic images on a CD-ROM.

Pica. A printing measurement unit used to specify line lengths, margins, columns, gutters, and so on. Equivalent to 12 points, or about 1/6 of an inch.

Pixel. A picture element, or the smallest addressable component of a displayable image. Used to describe resolution.

Plate. A thin, flexible sheet of metal, paper, or plastic used in offset printing. It contains a photographic reproduction of the page.

Point Size. The vertical measurement of type, equivalent to the distance between the highest ascender and lowest descender.

Point. A unit of measurement used in printing and typography that is roughly equivalent to 1/72 of an inch.

Portrait. Vertical orientation of a page or display. See Landscape.

Position stat. A photocopy or other reproduction of a halftone that is pasted onto a mechanical to show the printer how to crop and position the final image.

Posterization. A photographic effect in which the number of gray levels in an image is reduced to achieve a poster-like effect.

PostScript. A page description language developed by Adobe Systems Inc. and used by many laser printers and phototypesetters. See Page description language.

PostScript Clone. A page description language that emulates PostScript. In theory, a PostScript clone printer can produce any page that a true PostScript printer can produce.

Print Spooler. A program that temporarily stores a file to be printed until the output device is available.

Process Camera. A camera used in graphic arts to photograph mechanicals and create printing plates.

Process Colors. The four colors needed for four-color printing: yellow, magenta, cyan, and black. See Four-color printing.

Proof. A trial copy of a page or publication used to check accuracy. Also short for proofread, meaning to check for mistakes.

Protocol. A formal set of conventions governing format of data and control of information exchange between two communication devices.

RAM. See Random Access Memory.

Random Access Memory (RAM). Computer memory that can be read and changed. Data can be written to a particular location without having to sequence through previous locations. RAM is volatile, so all data is lost on power down.

Raster Graphics. Pictures sent to printer as bit maps (each element of picture is dot defined as black or white).

Raster-Image Processor (RIP). A piece of hardware that electronically prepares a page created on a computer system for output on an imagesetter or other device.

Read Only Memory (ROM). Computer memory containing fixed data that cannot be changed once programmed. Programming is accomplished during the manufacturing process.

Reflective Media. Print media, such as paper, that show images by reflecting light back to the eye.

Register Marks. Marks used to permit exact alignment of pages. Usually printed just outside the live area and then trimmed off. The standard register mark is a small circle with a cross inside.

Register. Precise alignment of printing plates or negatives.

Resolution. The density of dots or pixels on a page or display, usually measured in dots per inch. The higher the resolution, the smoother the appearance of text or graphics.

RGB. An abbreviation for Red, Green and Blue, the primary colors used in CRT display devices.

ROM. See Read Only Memory.

Scale. To change the size of a piece of artwork.

Scanner. A digitizing device that converts a piece of artwork into an electronic bit-map that can be loaded and manipulated by a software program. A means of converting hand-drawn art or photos into electronic form.

Screen. The pattern of dots used to make a halftone or tint. Halftone screens are measured in lines, equivalent to dots per inch. Tint screens are measured in percentages, with a 10-percent screen being very light and a 100-percent screen being totally black.

Screen Fonts. Digital typefaces used for screen display.

Separations. Transparencies or pages used for color reproduction. Each separation is used to reproduce a particular color. See Process color, four-color printing.

Sharpen. A filtering effect that enhances contrast around edges in an image.

Slide Scanner. An image scanner capable of scanning 35mm slides.

Small Computer Systems Interface (SCSI). An interface for connecting disks and other peripheral devices to computer systems. SCSI is defined by an American National Standards Institute (ANSI) standard and is widely used throughout the computer industry.

Soften. A filtering effect that decreases contrast in an image.

Solarization. A photographic effect achieved when a negative is briefly exposed to light. Some areas of the image are under-exposed, while others are over-exposed.

Spot Color. The use of one or more extra colors on a page, used to highlight specified page elements. Colors are usually specified as PMS codes. See Pantone Matching System.

Strip. To paste one piece of film, usually a halftone, into another piece of film containing a page. The film is then converted into a printing plate.

SyQuest. A removable hard disk system popular on the Macintosh. SyQuest disks can hold 44, 88, or 105 megabytes of data and are manufactured by several vendors.

Tagged Image File Format (TIFF). A graphics file format used to store color and gray-scale images.

Thermal Transfer. A technology used in many color printers in which ink or dye is transferred to the page using a heat process.

386. A computer system that uses the 80386 microprocessor from Intel.

Thumbnail. A rough layout of a page, usually used for planning purposes.

TIFF. See Tagged Image File Format.

Transmissive Media. Film-based media, such as 35 mm slides or transparencies, that require backlighting to be seen.

Transparency Scanner. An image scanner capable of scanning transparencies.

Typeface. A particular type design. See Font, Typeface Family.

VGA. Short for Video Graphics Array, a popular color display standard in the PC-compatible environment. See CGA, EGA, Hercules.

Virtual Memory. A hardware and software mechanism in which a hard disk is used as an extension of RAM.

Word Processor. A program used to enter, edit, and manipulate text.

Workstation. A full-featured desktop or deskside computer typically dedicated to a single person's use.

WYSIWYG. An acronym for What You See Is What You Get, meaning that text and graphics on a screen correspond closely to final printed output. Pronounced wizzy-wig.

Zoom. To view an enlarged (zoom in) or reduced (zoom out) portion of a page on screen.

*L*ist of Vendors

Adobe Systems Inc.
1585 Charleston Rd.
Mountain View, CA 94039
(415) 961-4400
Graphics software, printing software

Agfa Div. Miles Inc.
100 Challenger Rd.
Ridgefield Park, NJ 07660-2199
(201) 440-2500
Imagesetters, laser printers, scanners, film recorders

Aldus Corp.
411 First St. South, Suite 200
Seattle, WA 98104
(206) 622-5500
Page layout software, graphics software, presentation software

---

AVR Technology
71 E. Daggett Dr.
San Jose, CA 95134
(408) 434-1115
Scanners

Computer Support Corp.
15926 Midway Rd.
Dallas, TX 74244
(214) 661-8960
Graphics software

Corel Corp.
Corel Building, 1600 Carling
Ottawa, Canada, K1Z 7M4
(613) 728-8200
Graphics software

Eastman Kodak Co.
Rochester, NY 14650
(800) 242-2424
Scanners, color printers, graphics software, Photo CD

Frame Technology
1010 Rincon Circle
San Jose, CA 95131
(408) 433-1928
Page layout software

Hewlett-Packard
16399 W. Bernardo Dr.
San Diego, CA 92127
(619) 487-4100
Scanners, laser printers, color printers

Howtek Inc.
21 Park Ave.
Hudson, NH 03051
(603) 882-5200
Drum scanners

IBM Corp.
1133 Westchester Ave.
White Plains, NY 10604
(800) 431-2670
Computers, multimedia software

Iomega Corp.
1821 West 4000
South Roy, UT 84067
(801) 778-1000
Removable storage devices

Iris Graphics, Inc.
6 Crosby Dr.
Bedford, MA 01730
(617) 275-8777
Color printers

Leaf Systems
250 Turnpike Rd.
South Borough, MA 01772
(508) 460-8300
Slide/transparency scanners, digital cameras

Linotype-Hell Co.
425 Oser Avenue
Hauppauge, NY 11788
(516) 434-2000
Imagesetters, scanners

Macromedia
410 Townsend St., #408
San Francisco, CA
(415) 442-0200
Multimedia software

Matrox Electronic Systems, Ltd.
1055 St. Regis Blvd.
Dorval, Quebec Canada H9P2P4
(514) 685-2630
Color display boards

Micrografx Inc.
1303 Arapaho
Richardson, TX 75081
(214) 234 1769
Graphics software

Microsoft Corp.
One Microsoft Way
Redmond, WA 98052
(206) 882-8080
Page layout software, system software

Microtek Lab
680 Knox St.
Torrance, CA 90502
(800) 654-4160
Flatbed scanners, slide/transparency scanners

Mustek Inc.
17795-F Skypark Cir.
Irvine, CA 92714
(714) 833-7740
Hand-held scanners, flatbed scanners

Nikon Electronic Imaging
1300 Walt Whitman Rd.
Melville, NY 11747
(516) 547-4355
Slide scanners

Nisca Inc.
1919 Old Denton Rd. #104
Carrollton, TX 75006
(214) 242-9696
Hand-held scanners, flatbed scanners

Oce USA, Inc.

5450 N. Cumberland Ave.
Chicago, IL 60656
(800) 342-1766
Color printers

Optronics

7 Stuart Rd.
Chelmsford, MA 01824
(508) 256-4511
Drum scanners

Pantone Inc.

55 Knickerbocker Rd.
Moonachie, NJ 07074
(201) 935-5500
Color matching system

PixelCraft Corp.

P.O. Box 14467
Oakland, CA 94614-2467
(800) 933-0330
Flatbed scanners, slide/transparency scanners

QMS Inc.

1 Magnum Pass
Mobile, AL 36619
(205) 633-4300
Color printers

Quark Inc.

300 S. Jackson St., Suite 100
Denver, CO 80209
(303) 934-2211
Page layout software

Radius, Inc.
1710 Fortune Dr.
San Jose, CA 95131
(408) 434-1010
Color display systems

RasterOps
2500 Walsh Avenue
Santa Clara, CA 95051
(408) 562-4200
Color display systems, color printers

Scitex America Corp.
8 Oak Park Drive
Bedford, MA 01730
(617) 275-5150
Scanners, imagesetters

Screen USA
5110 Tollview Drive
Rolling Meadows, IL 60008
(708) 870-1960
Drum scanners

Sharp Electronics
Sharp Plaza
Mahwah, NJ 07430
(201) 529-8200
Flatbed scanners

Tamarack Technologies
1544 Centre Point Dr.
Milpitas, CA 95035
(800) 643-0666
Flatbed scanners

Tektronix Inc.

26600 SW Parkway
Wilsonville, OR 97070
(503) 685-2675
Color printers

3M Printing and Publishing Systems

3M Center Bldg. 223-2N-01
St. Paul, MN 55144
(612) 733-3497
Color printers

Umax Technologies

3170 Coronado Dr.
Santa Clara, CA 95054
(408) 982-0771
Flatbed scanners

Ventura Software Inc.

15175 Innovation Dr.
San Diego, CA 92128
(619) 673-7537
Page layout software

Xerox Corp.

Xerox Square
Rochester, NY 14644
(716) 423-5090
Digital copiers

ZSoft Corp.

450 Franklin Rd., #100
Marietta, GA 30067
(404) 428-0008
Graphics software

*I*ndex

VGA
  displays 27
Video digitizers 107, 112
Viewer
  command 45
Virtual memory
  turning on and off 42
  used by PhotoFinish 35

W

Wide Aperture
  option in blend filter 55
Width and Shape
  workbox 85
Window
  menu 40
Windows
  service bureau output 182
Word processors
  graphical 162

Z

Zoom
  command 70
  tool 80

Digital Photography: Pictures of Tomorrow

by John Larish
Micro Publishing Press
ISBN 0-941845-08-7 $27.95
Bookstore Distribution by Publishers Group West

This new book from Micro Publishing Press is an applications-oriented guide targeted at computer users interested in digital photography and electronic imaging. It explains the basics of digital photography and the process of using digital images in computer-generated publications. Numerous case studies show how users in various industries are already putting digital photography to work.

Whether you're an amateur photographer, desktop publisher, multimedia producer, or electronics hobbyist, you'll find this book to be a valuable resource.

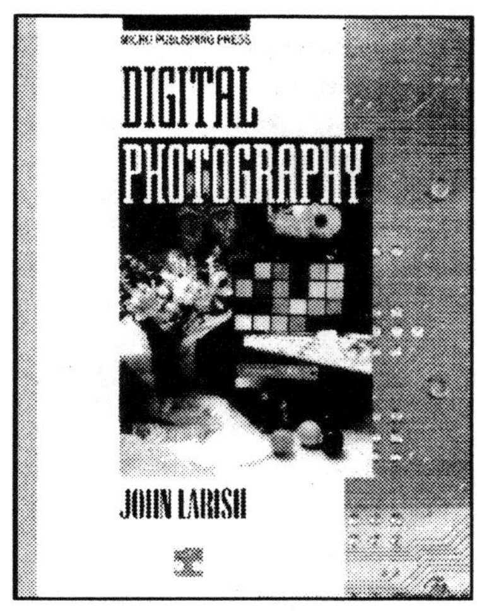

Key Topics

- Capturing and Storing Photographs
- Processing Images
- Creating Pages
- Producing Soft and Hard Copy
- Multimedia Applications

The Author

John Larish is the editor of *Electronic Photography News* and a former senior marketing staff member at Eastman Kodak Company.

- -

ORDER FORM

Please send ____copies of *Digital Photography: Pictures of Tomorrow*

❑ Enclosed is my check for $27.95 plus $3 shipping. (California residents add 8.25% sales tax.)

❑ Please charge my ❑ MasterCard ❑ Visa ❑ American Express

Number ____ Exp Date ________________

Signature ____

Name ____

Company____

Address ____

City ___________________________ State _______________ Zip _______________

Telephone ____

Remit to: Micro Publishing Press, 21150 Hawthorne Blvd. #104, Torrance, CA 90503 (310) 371-5787 Fax:(310) 542-0849

The CD ROM Book

by Les Cowan
Micro Publishing Press
ISBN 0-941845-12-5 $27.95
Bookstore Distribution by Publishers Group West

There is currently a vast hunger for information about CD-ROM, fueled by the growing number of products and the enormous marketing resources behind it. *The CD-ROM Book* clears up any possible confusion that users might have regarding formats, compatabilty with computers and software.

The book describes many specific ways in which people in a wide range of fields—including advertising, publishing, and commercial design—can use CD-ROM to make their jobs easier.

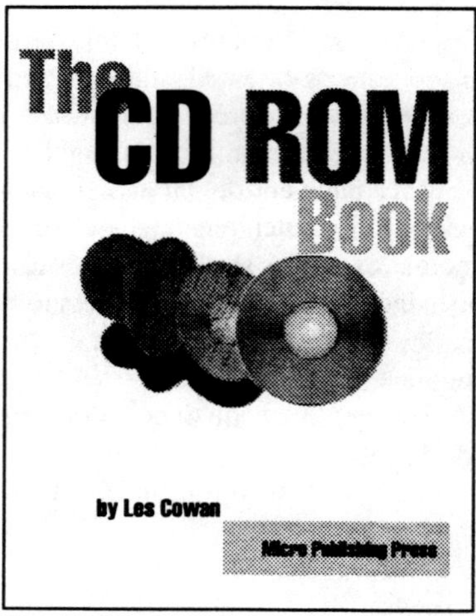

Key Topics

- Using CD-ROM with service bureaus
- Authoring software
- Working with disc-pressing firms
- Using with prepress software
- Case studies of the best ways to use and get the most from CD-ROMs.

The Author

Les Cowan is a Northern California based author and editor of the Northern California edition of *Micro Publishing News.*

ORDER FORM

Please send ____copies of *The CD ROM Book*

❏ Enclosed is my check for $27.95 plus $3 shipping. (California residents add 8.25% sales tax.)

❏ Please charge my ❏ MasterCard ❏ Visa ❏ American Express

Number ____ Exp Date _______________

Signature ____

Name ____

Company ____

Address ____

City _________________________________ State ________________ Zip _______________

Telephone ____

Remit to: Micro Publishing Press, 21150 Hawthorne Blvd. #104, Torrance, CA 90503 (310) 371-5787 Fax:(310) 542-0849

The Color Scanner Book

by Stephen Beale and James Cavuoto
Micro Publishing Press
ISBN 0-941845-11-7 $27.95
Bookstore Distribution by Publishers Group West

This new book from Micro Publishing Press is an applications-oriented guide targeted at computer users interested in color scanning and electronic imaging. It explains the basics of color scanning and the process of using scanners in computer-generated publications. Numerous examples show how users in various industries are using scanners to better their productions.

All people who use scanned images in their work will find this book to be a valuable resource.

Key Topics

- Scanning Images
- Hardware Requirements
- Photo Retouching Programs
- Tips for Producing The Best Scans
- Multimedia Applications

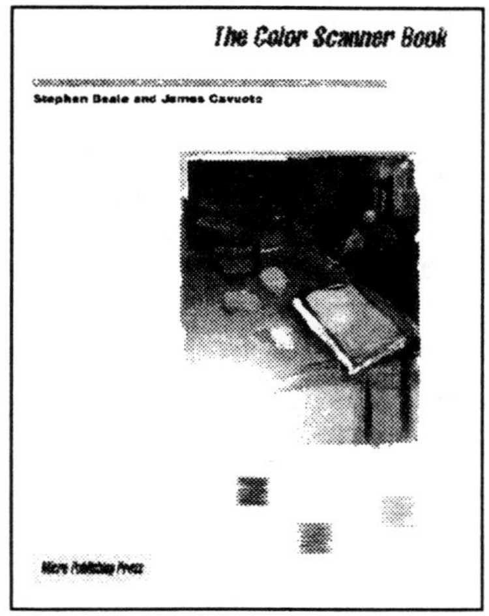

The Authors

James Cavuoto and Stephen Beale are recognized experts on desktop publishing and scanning. They serve as editors of the industry newsletter *Micro Publishing Report* and *Micro Publishing News.*

ORDER FORM

Please send ____copies of *The Color Scanner Book*

❑ Enclosed is my check for $27.95 plus $3 shipping. (California residents add 8.25% sales tax.)

❑ Please charge my ❑ MasterCard ❑ Visa ❑ American Express

Number ____ Exp Date __________________

Signature ____

Name ____

Company ____

Address ____

City _____________________________________ State __________________ Zip __________________

Telephone ____

Remit to: Micro Publishing Press, 21150 Hawthorne Blvd. #104, Torrance, CA 90503 (310) 371-5787 Fax:(310) 542-0849

Photo CD: Quality Photos at Your Fingertips

by John Larish
Micro Publishing Press
ISBN 0-941845-09-5 $27.95
Bookstore Distribution by Publishers Group West
Photo Trade Distribution by Saunders

Photo CD: Quality Photos at Your Fingertips is an informative introduction to Eastman Kodak's Photo CD, an exciting new technology that makes photographs available on a new form of compact disc. Aimed at computer users and photographers, this book offers everything you need to know to take advantage of Photo CD.

The marriage of traditional film and computer technologies promises to change the way we live, work, and play, providing new, interactive options in entertainment, education, and business. Photo CD is a bridge to the digital world, and this book is your gateway to this breakthrough technology.

Key topics include:

- Uses for Photo CD
- How Photo CD works
- Printing and enhancing Photo CD images
- Publishing with Photo CD
- Legal implications of Photo CD
- The compact disc family
- The future of Photo CD

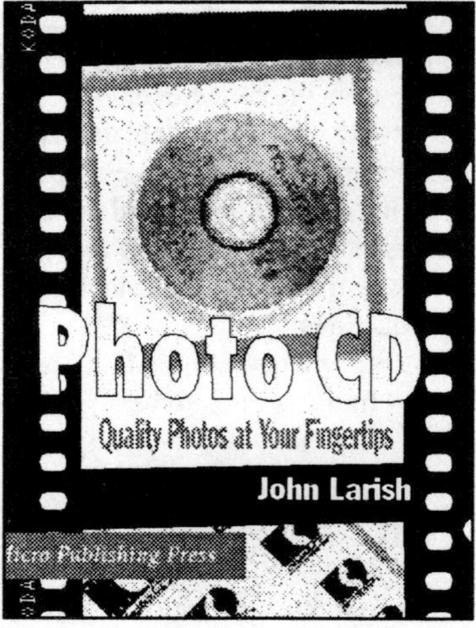

The Author

John Larish is the editor of *Electronic Photography News* and a former senior marketing staff member at Eastman Kodak Company.

ORDER FORM

Please send ____copies of *Photo CD: Quality Photos at Your Fingertips*

❑ Enclosed is my check for $27.95 plus $3 shipping. (California residents add 8.25% sales tax.)

❑ Please charge my ❑ MasterCard ❑ Visa ❑ American Express

Number ____ Exp Date _______________

Signature ____

Name ____

Company ____

Address ____

City _________________________________ State ______________ Zip _______________

Telephone ____

Remit to: Micro Publishing Press, 21150 Hawthorne Blvd. #104, Torrance, CA 90503 (310) 371-5787 Fax:(310) 542-0849